MW01140962

CHAPBOOKS BY SMOKING LUNG PRESS

Poetry
Her Own Rituals by Lori Maleea Acker
Forgetting the Rest Beyond Blue by Shane Book
Just in from Fun City by Adam Chiles
Songs I Use to Chase Rye by Brad Cran
The Nature of Women, Soup and Sky by Aubri Keleman
Solomon's Wives by Carla Funk
A Promise of Motion by Mike Lane
Sometimes Gay Means Happy by Billeh Nickerson
Here You Learn Not To by Gillian Wigmore
Lost In All Directions by Kerri Embry
What Leaves Us by Ryan Knighton
Hundred Block At Nine by Lyle Neff
Eating Dirt by Karen Solie

Fiction
Can I Buy You A Drink? by Debra Miller
The Gull by Andrew Musgrave
Some Girls Do by Teresa McWhirter

Creative Non-Fiction
One Damn Thing After Another by Barclay Brick Blair
When I Say Nine O'clock I Need To Mean It by Jenny Durrant

Forthcoming Poetry
Stillborn at the Cornerhouse Cafe by Brad Cran
Season of Strangers by Chris Hutchinson
Thrills, Chills and Aspirin Pills by Billie Livingston

HAMMER&Tongs

A SMOKING LUNG ANTHOLOGY
Edited by Brad Cran

Hammer & Tongs
Copyright © 1999 by Smoking Lung Press

All rights reserved. No part of this publication may be reproduced or transmitted in any form by any means, electronic or mechanical, including photocopying, recording, or any information storage and retrieval system, without permission in writing from the publisher, except by a reviewer, who may use brief excerpts in a review.

First Edition

Published in 1999 by
Smoking Lung Press
#103-1014 Homer Street
Vancouver BC
V6B 2W9

Distributed through
Arsenal Pulp Press
#103-1014 Homer Street
Vancouver BC
V6B 2W9
www.arsenalpulp.com

Cover photo by Mandelbrot
Cover design and interior layout by Brad Cran

Author Photos from left to right and top to bottom: Adam Chiles by Shane Book, Teresa McWhirter by Greg Treadwell, Carla Funk by Anon, Aubri Aleka Keleman by Shane Book, Shane Book by Brad Cran, Chris Hutchinson by Teresa McWhirter, Billie Livingston by Kevin Clark, Karen Solie by Gary Anderson, Lori Maleea Acker by Shane Book, Ryan Knighton by Tracy Rawa, Billeh Nickerson by Mandelbrot, Brad Cran by Mandelbrot

All the authors in this book originally published their sections (or variations of their sections) in chapbook form with Smoking Lung Press.

Printed and Bound in Canada

CANADIAN CATALOGUING IN PUBLICATION DATA:

Main entry under title:
Hammer & Tongs

Poems.
ISBN 1-894442-00-8

1. Canadian poetry (English)—British Columbia—Vancouver.
2.Canadian poetry (English)—20th century.* I. Cran, Brad, 1972-
PS8295.7.V35H35 1999 C811*.5408'0971133 C99-911041-1
PR9198.3.V32H35 1999

CONTENTS

INTRODUCTION

In the mid-nineties the possibilities of publication and exposure for aspiring poets were limited to writing contests, the few literary journals scattered across the country, open mikes and a new phenomenon called slam poetry. Writing contests consistently proved to be a waste of money, literary journals were almost always unread by anyone outside the literary community, open mikes were generally unbearable and slam poetry quickly defined itself as more game than art. There was no local public and printed forum for an aspiring poet who had a substantial body of work but was not yet ready to publish in book form—and for many of us this was the most exciting stage of apprenticeship.

In 1996, in a bar in Victoria, Shane Book, Barclay Brick Blair and I decided to publish individual collections of our own work under an imprint which would become Smoking Lung Press. We commissioned a tattooist to create a logo, approached a printer for a line of credit, invited four other writers to join us in publication and it was official: we were publishers.

On the night of our first launch we waited in the large room of the Open Space Gallery in Victoria as a few people trickled in. An hour later the room filled with three hundred people and we'd already sold the majority of our books and made a trip to the liquor store to restock the bar. Our need for a local printed and public forum was fulfilled and within a week manuscripts for our second launch began flowing in.

Since that night Smoking Lung has published fourteen more chapbooks and put together two launch parties and numerous smaller shows throughout Vancouver, now incorporating visual artists and singer-songwriters. The object of these shows has been to break down the barriers not only between styles of poetry but between all genres of the arts. The result is an eclectic group of artists who come together to share their audience and their art in a forum that has no mandate other than quality work. On many occasions I've been approached by people who have said they came to see the band or a particular artist but had now bought their first book of poetry. This is Smoking Lung at its best.

I first heard the expression "hammer & tongs" from Adam Chiles and it is a term I will always associate with Smoking Lung, partly as something we've often said before a sip of beer but also as representative of an ideology of poetry and the arts that is the common bond between the diversity of voices within this book. Whether it is Aubri Keleman reinventing Jack Horner or Ryan Knighton spotting Descartes at Kentucky Fried Chicken, in this collection you will see and hear many different styles and voices of poetry but always a poetry that is a product of craft.

Over the last three years Smoking Lung has grown from a bar room discussion, to a chapbook press, to an impresario for the arts and now to a book publisher. It has defined itself through the diversity and strength of poetry and art being produced in British Columbia. In many ways it is out of control and I wouldn't want it any other way.

Brad Cran
Publisher

So while the parish priest at her bedside
Went hammer and tongs at the prayers for the dying
And some were responding and some crying
I remembered her head bent towards my head,
Her breath in mine, our fluent dipping knives—
Never closer the whole rest of our lives.

Seamus Heaney
from "Clearances"

HAMMER & TONGS

HER OWN RITUALS

Lori Maleea Acker

WITH MY FATHER THEN AND NOW

Along the smaller streets, passing down through
fields once named when driving mornings, quiet
from the early hour, into school, my love
for my father dwindled into subtle
embarrassment, a slow, studied hate.
How long did his face fall, a reflection,
green from the dashboard light, into my lap,
into my hands, the line of his jawbone
one more place I could cross? When it ended,
I don't remember. These days, his slight heart
beats awkward, and a bruised breath of mine travels
stronger daily, my chest to his. Perhaps
by giving this, the windows of his car
will steam, reflect my love only, growing,
more a strange, strong mineral every day.

MECHANIC

During the day there is work, the forcing of metal
against metal in the engine practice rooms,
a net of diagrams catching him endless, scoring
the tender parts of his fingers. He imagines double hulled tankers,
burrowing safer through swells because of his thought patterns,
the way his mind contains a series of clicks, the snap of a fuse.
He holds a hovering puzzlement over the nature
of explosion, a towering piston rod falling exact into place.
At night, the sound of a two-stroke, heart-chugging
for six and a half hours with only the smallest drop of oil.
The whir has often driven him out of his apartment,
falling against the sidewalk in a random jog, his feet
straining to break clockwork night. Perhaps one evening
he ends up, astonished, the edge of the government dock,
railings inches from him. He leans against the shedding paint,
dry flakes of it marking a bright line across his chest.
Perhaps it is then he tugs the belt, the buttons aside.
Even this movement, when he begins, knees bent and resting
against the first wooden bar of the railing, has a cadence, a stroke.
He can hear the tide washing in over the rocks below,
his breath pushing out over the sea, his head bent down,
hand a machine working against softness, working away from night.
He closes his eyes, whirls, and leans hard against a railing,
which holds him, immutable, the lap of water not enough
to transfer through the wood beams, long, wide planks
of the dock. And then finally, he is leaning out
over the water, springing from himself, falling to the water,
a glow against the dark water, so thoroughly
there is only a drop left to touch, some kind of reaffirmation,
an allowance given for awkward beats. It is then
he cries, bringing his hand to his mouth,
which tastes also of metal, of oil.
Perhaps it is then,
he realizes there is no place for men who cannot leave,
ones who attempt to stammer like wings out from under
their beating lives, falling softly every time.

LETTER TO CELESTE, FALL 1997

Every day, I cannot bear to put pen to paper for you,
and so instead, a curving plane of letters
encircles every bus I ride, every street I walk down.
I fear the sight of my love for you, stuttering
across crosswalks, a small rift behind the wheels of cars.
Come back and I will show you how to divine my path from house to sea
and back again. I cannot break out of this circle; like birds
following me, the syllables knocking against the thin skin over my heart.
As a measure against the approaching cold, do you remember our dance
together, in the kitchen, spinning desperate into the host's hallway,
the dinner party a subtle animal in the next room?
You words of love so thin, so ready to leave me.
Tonight there is frost and the crickets have finally fallen silent.
In my palms, I hold the imaginary, the shift of your mouth,
your thumbprint against the curve of a glass.
I wanted words to be my messengers, my tenderness,
the ones that uncover and show. Instead they are my demons, they unskin
me, as one would a plum, and I follow them, *a kind of sad dance*
that curves my breath against the edge of my world.

Italics taken from the poem Pavane, by Jack Gilbert

It was after a day when the wind fell against him so hard,
he felt at any moment, he could be blown down the street,
held gravely to the strongest thing he could find
wherever he was: a street lamp, the large woman with the overcoat
hulking in front of him, the grate in the pavement, beneath
which flashed strange orange lights and low voices.
It was at home during a pause between commercials,
a small moment of blank space between him and his lover
that was not filled the way noise had begun
to fill everything else. They had not spoken for three days,
the food low, the telephone silent, his hand tight
around the arm of the couch. The wind rattled the doorknob,
he turned toward the sound. It was then she said, There are things, love,
which even you should be able to give me.
He had run dry quite a time ago, having consumed the last
of the bread, the mustard, the milk gone bad at the back of the fridge.
He craved her in a way that could not be described. His hands
anchored to everything he grasped. The furniture held
imprints of his fingers, bare spots where he rubbed
at stubborn patterns that refused to leave his eyes.
The wind circled the house, strong and cutting in
at edges of their lives. He glanced at her during an ad for comforters,
wished for something which would carry weight,
hold water, felt himself empty and lacking of all
he knew she desired. Come now Margaret, he longed to say,
or is it Chloe? Perhaps he had never known.
The wind licked in the corners of the room, an eddy
passed around his shoes and lifted the laces, and then he knew.
At that very moment there was no doubt.
He lifted the corner of his shirt away from his body
and raised it so one nipple was visible on his chest.
When he offered it to her, it seemed she almost understood
the gesture. She bent her head, dark against his chest
after a winter of small light, and took the button of it in her mouth.
Nothing is all that is left, he murmured, and that is all I can give you now,
though without reserve, though without reserve.

HER OWN RITUAL

After she has settled his body
in the bow, pushed the dinghy
away from the sand and begun to row,
there is no noise. She paddles
softly, the way he taught her,
as if they were trying only to curve
closer to an otter, a harbour seal, ears
flat against its head.

When she has gotten up speed, moving
away from the curl of the bay
so quickly, she can see the beach shrink
she turns, loosens the painter
from where it has slipped under her father,
gathers it long in her arms.

She wraps the free end around the girth
of his stomach several times, pulling
tighter until she hears an escape
of air from his lips, feels his body
settle softly into the hull.

She ties the end of the rope onto the cleat in the stern,
a bowline knot, the one he taught her
that knows its own weakness.
She finds the pages of newspaper she slipped into her pockets
as she left the house with him, crumples
each piece slowly, watching her hands
turn dark from the ink.

Though she no longer rows,
the water slips past them.
When she is finished, the boat
is suddenly smaller, filled with him
and the bulk of the paper
unfolding around them both.

cont...

Standing, she removes her shoes.
In her hand she holds the matches,
fingers poised as if trying
to speak some language, follow
the weave of a certain knot she is reminded of
by the tangle of hair on his forehead.

The first match does not catch, the wind
off the water licking into her hand.
The second she cups down low against her body
and the hull of the boat.
She waits until it hooks onto the paper,
watches it flounder in such bright light,
the flames grabbing at the dry of his hair.

When she jumps, she is careful
not to use the edge as leverage,
lets her body fall away. She surfaces
a small distance from him, turns to see
the boat already bright with flames, rocking
slightly with the force of the fire.

FORGETTING THE REST
BEYOND BLUE
Shane Book

For Colleen,

Thanks for coming out

to the launch

& Best,

SB

VAN '99

BLUE JOURNAL

1.

Laid out in bed, bulked down under cotton,
skin simmering, simmering,

my chest, a field of small bubbles.
I swallow whole the small white songs

and the valium comes, humming its slant hymns.
The second hand on the wall clock sleeps

and the swaying drapes sleep and the soft light
of afternoon through the window sleeps,

and regret ends. Nothing moves, but if something
does, it does. The plick, plick of a thumbnail

splitting an insect, bubbles popping
under my thumbs, one by one. Healthy

or not, veins stay blue in the skin.
Clear liquid on my thumbs, to my lips,

cyst water, cyst water. Disease is not original,
essence is a long tunnel, essence is blue.

Recovering from Shingles; Maple House, Accra, Ghana, 1984.

2.

Early morning on the Madawaska river:
air cool, breezeless, mist clings to the flat

black, an insistent voice in the head.
Upstream, rapids thunder on, oblivious

to argument. Following the river, a Heron,
quiet grey wedge waving past the green pines,

whispers to no one in particular:
The world wakes, then circles,

The world dies again. A thin white man
stands naked on a rock ledge, shivers

like the birches that sliver light into the forest.
Arms swinging, body rocking heel to toe,

he pauses, knees bent, then springs
into morning with one breath. Mist slips,

rapids drone on. By its beak, Heron pulls
the new day along. Great bird, great blue.

Dad taking morning swim, canoe trip; near Quadville, Ontario, 1991.

3.

The moon moults
in the West African sky.

The stars slow dance alone
in their death beds.

Breakers bludgeon the beach.
A slight wind continues

its grain by grain business
with no visible dread.

The one sure thing about Form,
the masters tell us, is that it changes.

Except, I add, when you're thirteen
and relaxing with friends and a crate

of stolen Beaujolais. Then, landscape
really is an abstraction, then, it's all smiles.

Smiling as long as we can hold it.
Blue tinge beginning in the night sky.

Just before being arrested; Labadi Beach, Accra, Ghana, 1983.

4.

The river spools out through the granite
channel like a tongue,

gentle, pushing its stream of dark syllables.
Mosquitoes fuzz the cedars. A crow jump-cuts

the cross breezes, hoping someone slips up.
Late Spring in the Opeongo Hills

and the world glides by on a slip stream.
Well that's how it feels in a beat-up canoe,

maiden of the near-miss, vessel of our dumb luck.
That's how it feels in the calm patches,

between the rapids of this watery life.
Sometimes you catch a break, the world bats

its blue eye, and you take it, and paddle on.
But make no mistake, hombre.

Everything wakes to a thirst of its own making.
Everything dulls in its shine.

Shortly before wrecking canoe in Rifle Chute; near Griffith, Ontario, 1979.

5.

Lying face up in the squeak, shuff and rumble,
a line of rivets joyrides the length of my spine.

All around, voices talk the talk
of the long waiting. A cotton sarong

bulges through slits in the seat above.
This being human is a guest house,

say the Sufis, whoever shows up, be grateful,
take them in. But what if you're on the floor

of a third class train from Rangoon,
what if you're waiting down here in the dark

and crying of that other world?
Thirteen more hours to Mandalay: bleating goats,

squawking chickens, smell of piss, smell of fear.
Beneath us all, it's metal on metal,

hard sparks going off along a steel river.
Oh Blue we're counting on you, to get us there.

Recovering from dysentery; southern Myanmar, 1985.

FALL

Starting first with the rug, spreading it flat
on the grass. Taking the tables and chairs next.
Arranging it all as he had found them: the books,
she and the neighbour, as though they were still
in the room. Watching the wind flip the corners of the rug,
the branches of the tree, moving. Thinking of the neighbour,
whether the fruit that fell across the property line
belonged to anyone, now. Wondering why
he'd never noticed before. Smelling the damp chill
of the season. Wondering if Fall could be considered
an answer to greed, an answer to anything,
the empty room, the house, returning to it. Forgetting
the neighbour. Trying to remember the way it was.
Freezing instead her face in his mind, especially the eyes,
that primary colour. Trying to remember the details
of the room, forgetting the rest beyond blue.
Taking the boxes of books out to the yard.
Positioning the shelf on the grass,
just behind the table, the books on the shelf,
placing them there, trying to remember the order:
the Chekhov, the Proust, the Montaigne.
Returning with the paintings, not the Turner, not the Braque,
but the Constable, the Watteau,
laying them out on the table. Tipping the gasoline can.
Soaking the paintings, the table, the chairs,
well and through. Reaching the books, finally.
Seeing the large leather dictionary. Imagining
the pages, how they would look in flame.
Wondering what it was like before language,
before the word *yes*. Imagining fire,
the first acquiescence to pain.

DUST

Our last night together, in the small hours, she took me by the hand
        into the bathroom, ran the water,
and soaped me down. Her hands moved over my skin, separately,
        though in concert, like two people
who know each other well but are not lovers, slow-dancing together
        in the farthest corner of the bar

for the last song of the evening, that time of night everyone alone dreads.
        But we were not,
at that moment, in a bar—we were in a bathroom of the Barclay Hotel
        in Vancouver, on a warm evening
in late July, which I admit sounds wonderful, though if I had
        the night to do over, I might have avoided

bathing in that small white tiled bathroom, so similar to a room
        last December, in a hospital
in Winnipeg, where outside the north wind blows the snow in the
        formations of whatever snow dreams
it might be, where my grandfather in the hospital bed, when asking
        what's new in the world,

looks to the window, as if questioning not me but the snow swirling past,
        a man trying to understand
how the cancer comes on, almost imperceptibly, as in, One day it's just
        there in my chest, as in,
How does it happen, Shane, can you tell me? And because I have no
        answer for that question,

I respond with another, What about getting you a shower, Grandpa? And
        then he turns to me,
and I am slipping his moccasins over the cracked skin of his feet,
        topographical maps bearing the marks
of the places he's been, baby shoes in Boston, brown feet on the sandy
        banks of the Red River,

soft leather brogues on the cold streets of Sault Ste. Marie. Then I shift
        his legs, spindly after weeks

cont...

in bed, and the green cotton gown rides up, revealing the place where
  the clear tube leaves him,
snakes down into the plastic sack, browning with the waste of his body.
  He's so light that with one arm

I lift him, and he pauses, arms hanging over my shoulders, and looks
  around the room with what I imagine
is wonder at the sudden uprightness of the world. And then we are
  walking slowly, in step
with each other, down the hospital corridor, one of his arms over my
  shoulder, the other on the cart

that holds the oxygen canister, and with one hand I steady the cart, in the
  other the bag of piss
swings, and I think of those times in my childhood, grocery shopping with
  my mother,
when she let me push the cart, my hand beside hers on the metal bar, how I
  would concentrate

so hard, that this might be one thing important, one thing to help, as I am
  helping now, moving down
the hallway with my grandfather, and as we pass the open doorways I
  notice he does not look in,
exactly, but pauses almost imperceptibly before the large flat diamonds of
  light on the floor,

the harsh light of a prairie winter coming through the windows in patients'
  rooms, and if it is true
that what is captured in the mind remains the same, then perhaps what he
  hesitates over on the polished
grey floors are the prairie winters of his youth. Without asking, I have no
  way of knowing this,

and because I know that for him just moving is tiring enough I
  am silent, my mind returning
to the light of his past as I have held it since tenth-grade history class, not
  flat and steady but flickering
black and white in those films from the thirties—the prairie a broad dusty
  tabletop full of ramshackle

cars, jerking across the screen, faces furrowed like the empty
        fields, tire marks
left in the chaos of dust. In truth, I watched little else of those films,
        preferred instead to whisper
with my friends, but there was one time when the screen held us all, a
        close-up of a boy, our age,
in flat cap and britches, scowling into the camera—mad as hell to be
        lining up for bread when
just last year his dad's acres spanned whole continents of wheat in his
        mind. But if my grandfather's youth
was that boy I'll never know, for even at this late stage in his life it is old
        time prairie pride

that prevents him from halting for more than a quick breath at the first
        diamonds of light his skin
has felt in weeks. Pride for the old woman who spends her days yelling at
        the nurses for more
food. Pride for the man who complains loudly the doctors are poisoning
        him. Pride for the woman

who calls out to a family that never comes. If it's for anyone I think it's
        for these people my grandfather's
pause is as slight as a whispered secret, the kind a lover breathes late at
        night in a bath, for some reason
you can never know, when her hands take hold of the soft sponge, the bar
        of soap, and in the bald light

of the bathroom's too-small tub, she rises up out of the water, runs the
        sponge along the length
of your arms, leaning into you, so that her breasts swing out close to your
        lips and you think
of taking a nipple in your mouth, but giving way instead to some sense of
        decorum, decide against it,

and for this, then, or some other reason, she smiles, just as my grandfather
        smiles now when
I help him stand in the white tiled shower room, after I've removed the
        green gown, and he leans
into me, and the water splashes down, soaking my hair, his hair, my shirt
        and his naked body.

cont...

And when I pick up the soap and begin, my hands moving over him
        slowly, to the places he points,
I try to imagine the way he might do it. I do not ask how it feels when I
        rub the dark bruises
made by daily needles in the crooks of his arms, do not ask because this is
        simply a job to be done,
the way those prairie people in the flickering movies of our minds did the
        things they had to, silently,
to stay alive. And my hands, graceful in their ignorance, move over his
        body, not knowing
this is a rehearsal for something they will witness later, in a hotel room in
        Vancouver, when the hands

of another person will dance over my body, because this was right now,
        and right now the knowledge
my hands carry of how this dance will disappear and return in my life is
        hidden well enough
to keep us both, the old man and me, still moving in my mind, two
        dancers in the smallest hours,

in the farthest corner of a dimly lit bar, our slow turning in one spot a
        kind of contemplation,
of wheat fields, water, snow, skin and dust.

JUST IN FROM
FUN CITY

Adam Chiles

ASK THE DUST

If I were to tell you that I left my skin
on the beach of Algeciras and walked finally naked
aboard the ferry, and in this act, knew a freedom
that comes with crossing an ocean between
two continents, you might call me a fool,
but you are not me, and in my belligerence I will
tell you that I left my history on the Spanish shore
gladly and without remorse, wanting only
the indefinite sky and the slow rising of Tangiers.
It doesn't matter that I would find little
in this town except a succession of days under
a tired sun, and faces burnt to a permanent anger.
I did not come here to kiss the hotel mirror and
claim some false arrival. And to say the man
smoking his clay pipe outside my window appeared
to me one night as a prophet, is to lie.
If I told you I had a revelation on the train
to Casablanca, that it came from a boy barely old enough
to travel alone, you would not believe me,
you would not believe that such a child might share
his faith with a stranger and that we knelt there
on the carriage floor, our faces breathing
a simple dust the feet have known for centuries.
But to walk into some forgotten neighbourhood of
Tangiers is to understand why a man might surrender
what he knows for a little truth, and why
I found myself sitting in a small room above the
medina listening to such a man whose only wisdom
now, was in the bright madness of his eye, staring
like that character in his story, the collector
last seen screaming his way back to the desert.

IN RESPONSE TO "FALL"
for Shane Book

I've been watching you carry out your life
all afternoon, starting with the rug, slowly building
rooms across your drive, carefully placing things
in order, the lampshade by the table, the books
inside their shelves. How the lawn appears to offer you
a green relief from the cold kitchen tiles.
You move each chair with grace, as if preparing
for a life opposite to pain, you lay dish after dish
on the dinner table, humming as you go, oblivious
to the empty settings, the afternoon light, its red
glowing off your knives. You drag everything out
but the curtains, those you leave behind to hang,
a final line of defense against a darkness
only the beaten man can know. And I think of your wife
now, heading off across the plains, her eyes burning
for the Atlantic, another man's face in your windshield,
both of them, quiet as Billings. The American highway:
an approach to night. Their car beams on for the horizon.
Perhaps they imagine you behind them, already gone, not there
drunk in the yard on bourbon, where you are singing now
not humming, as you move through the furniture,
match in hand, searching I suppose for a Cuban cigar.

A MAN CONSIDERS THE SEASONS

1.

Sometimes, while going about his life
he might buy an apple for no particular reason,
prompted only by a small thirst, he could be
strolling up Oxford Street with it, quite happy,
and think little of the splendid beauty
this fruit means. But taste has a way of taking him
back to a place; an orchard on the slopes
of the Okanagan Valley, the warmth of late summer
and the contingencies of love. He might remember that.
Walking home, one evening, exhausted by the day,
wanting nothing more than the rest her body offers.
This fruit makes it possible. Reminds him of those
days, wondering if the weight of the apple sack
resembles the weight she carries.

2.

Winter is a pure season. Like the Arctic Hare
whose coat changes with the light, a miracle fur,
that new growth the body recognizes on waking.
Like the soul. The fine accomplishment of solitude.
What a child discovers in the breast, and is silent.
He remembers such a place; a clearing in the woods
on Bowen Island, watching his wife feed their daughter
under the pines and sensing the gladness of things
about them. It is the private act that pleases him,
how life is altered and remains the same. Defined
by the shelter the body is. The way certain things
enter and depart without disturbing
the clarity of this surrounding.

THE CATHEDRAL

is empty, they warned me
but the darkness moves inside
and whispers from the shadows
like barely opened eyes, watch
the heat as it runs down the city.
Vendors are cooking in the square
as children peel from the hot corners,
picking their way through ruins,
feeling nothing but fear
crawl in their minds, like animals
biting the air, digesting silence.
They mine the streets with their hands
cupping the sun, as noon blisters
in Managua, paralyzing time.
The cathedral is haunted by voices,
by the sound of children beating
against dark walls and columns,
its belly aching with the memory
of spirits, the quiet burns
of confession, and the still existing
life in cracks and hiding places.
Where the sky drips through open
windows, ceiling gaps and holes,
and daylight falls like hot dust
into the chapel's throat, like sand
spitting from the sun,
the dark swallows everything,
holding in its rotten breath
the hungry creep and shuffle.
Men that sting the emptiness
with their eyes, feeding
desires that draw in the night.
They wait for the shade, as creatures
wait and listen for things approaching.
The cathedral is empty, they warned me.
But I feel the nerves itch
as they swarm inside, the buzzing
of tongues that taste my body
stepping through the dark.

ALMOST BLUE
after Chet Baker

He has sat in this hotel room for hours
the remote in one hand, bourbon in the other.
Beyond hope, he tells himself, is to regret nothing.
The bottle helps. He grips the neck, holding it vertical to his lips.
A trademark. Like Jackson Pollock who preferred
wood to the delicacy of brushes. He flicks
through the stations enjoying this control.
The images do not matter, it is his ability to move
that comforts him. He listens to the American Navy
boys clomping down the corridor outside his room,
they have been to the Uptown bar and have returned
with only two girls. Soon, he thinks, the fighting
will begin. Consider the painting on the wall
above the television set, its colours turned yellow
from smoke. The impermanence of that summer
is another form of betrayal. Like the slow failure
of his marriage. The way his movements in those
last days appeared to imitate some previous event,
as if his body had almost forgotten its reason for
being there, but still grasped, in brief moments,
a particular truth. Like that painting which still
contains the ghost of itself. He listens
to the girls bang down the stairwell and thinks of
Chet Baker in his final years, straining his entire
body into song. Not his inability to reach
the melody but the melody made beautiful by defeat.
He lies on his bed, lifting the bottle to his lips,
the night continuing, the girls back on Government Street.

FATHER

His father walks ahead of him, drawn by the mystery
of his youth, fascinated by houses, by these particular
fields, these hedges, wanting this fruit. He stops to taste
the brambles on his tongue, marvelling at the way they bleed,
each one a cousin to memory. "See," he says, turning to
his son, his hands cupped, "I picked these berries as a boy,
taste one." His son studies the spilt juices collecting
in his father's palms. He imagines being held this way,
seconds after birth, the redness in those hands the same
red his father knew then, pacing the corridors, fingers
singing with blood. He takes one of the berries and crushes
it with his teeth. A kind of sacrament, he thinks, the way
his father offers him this clarity the mouth knows
when it bursts the skin and tastes, for the first time, the
liquor of a primary world.

IN THIS HOUR
for Amanda

What is it that keeps a man from sleep at 3am
convinced of nothing anymore, and feeling nothing
but the dread tick of his own presence?
Is such a moment the slow autumn of the soul?
If, in this hour, he bows with the silent
resignation of a Benedictine monk, and kneels
as that man in some abbey of his making,
is it enough? And if he answers yes, is it possible
the sound of a car disappearing is not the sound of failure
but the quiet advancement of his mind?
He thinks of these things lying on a hotel bed
with a woman he will soon leave, listening
to the steady effort of a snowplough pushing its way
through the storm, a kind of dumb persistence,
like his attempt to resist the morning,
that sad glimmer the street lamps rehearse
for the night.
             Once, he proposed to a woman
in a blizzard and though he could barely find the road,
continued steering with one hand, the other
sure between her thighs. Perhaps it was
the snow's insistence that drove him to speak
as if something this soluble demanded fixing,
and maybe in that moment he believed
in every word he said, as if his mind was tuned
to the car, and the woman's silence
was the silence of achievement. And maybe it is possible
to find a truth in the dim light of this room
he lies in, just as it seemed possible in that car,
that words could bring about their meaning,
that stone is not the final measure of the heart.

STAIR
for djuna

This is how a stair grows
and how you begin to make
the first step through space.
This is how it feels
to think of angles
and the landing, and
how you remember them
as a child running up to your bed.
Every step comes back to you
one by one, every inch
leads into your past,
where you have carried ladders
to climb out of the ruins
and found the stairs beginning,
to think of banisters
moving firmly through the air
and the sound of footsteps,
imagine the stair,
dreaming of a giant spiral
and the way your mind spins
nails and boards to the next floor,
how you conquer space
with a flying hammer
and build a staircase
out of the blow, how
you feel every step
pulled like an accordion
from your body and how
the book of codes has taught you
this art of ascension
is the way a stair grows
and follows the figures
that rise inside you.

SONGS I USE TO CHASE RYE

Brad Cran

IMPERFECTION

Your beauty is best
after I cum in my lover.
When her breasts are sacks
of flesh, her taste
stale on my tongue.

This is my drunken impudence.
This is my beer belly.
This is my bloody fist.
This is my back street tattoo.
This is my lack of radiance.

This woman lying beside me
making you beautiful.

ABANDONMENT
for Patrick

Ready to go to her now as if he were the only one
who felt loss. Carrying in his hand a limp pheasant
with a broken neck. He had abandoned her
in early spring, with the stupidity of an overfed hunter
on the way to a kill. Now sated in everything but her
he builds a fire and says her name
as if she would finally be the one.
This, she thinks, is the last time,
there will never again be a good enough reason.
A dead bird plucked raw in the laundry sink,
coals smouldering on the fire,
and the calm he thinks he feels now
between seasons.

WINTER IN A SEASIDE HOME

Mornings are the worst. Dropping
your feet onto the cold hardwood
floor. Wondering if it's worth
the trouble: getting dressed, a cup of coffee,
finishing yesterday's paper but it's another
world far from the daily chores.
Dragging your ass through the yard,
shovel in hand, clearing out the drive
until the next snowfall. Close by
the ocean moves, salt and seaweed,
a flying gull, perhaps a pod of whales
off the point but that doesn't matter
now. All that's left you carry inside
and there is just enough time to split
the kindling for the evening fire
that you will build with care,
watching the flames, cracking
the bottle of rye you had always
hidden from her inside
your wool socks and you think
better that she left now,
better in the dead of winter,
love being the solitary occupation
that it is.

HITCHING

Catching a ride with a truck driver
heading to your hometown
is like reeling in a marlin
but it's the string of pan fries
that keeps you going.
Maybe you get lucky,
hook an overage X-hippie
driving a Beemer,
wanting to talk glory days.
Maybe he'll ask
when your last meal was,
slip you some cash and tell you
to keep the faith,
keep on rollin'
and you know you have
given him something
and you don't
feel so bad casting out your thumb,
flashing your smile,
wanting to throw stones
at the drivers as they slip away,
their eyes still pools
far from where you think
you're going.

DEATH OF A FRIEND BY OVERDOSE

He looked passed out, too many pills and whiskeys
and I wanted to pull a jiffy marker from the kitchen drawer, draw a moustache
on his face and call out to the rest, come quick, look
what Jeff's done now, the dumb-ass is all blue and cold and dead.
Last week he pissed in my sink full of dishes. Now this?
We should shave his eyebrows and tie his shoelaces together,
strip him naked and Saran Wrap him to a stop sign,
take his picture to stick on the refrigerator,
or just soak his hand in warm water. Can't corpses still piss?
Maybe we should put him in a shopping cart and push him
to his parent's doorstep and ring the bell then run,
leave a note saying: *Sorry but we could never stop him anyhow,*
in fact we loved him for excess. Keep him like this it's all he's become.
We'd love to stay but our stars are burning fast and dumb.

PATTERNS OF LEAVES

It's the lack of sadness that makes you want to cry.
No emotion or brother to hug. When you scream
the sky turns black and without stars.
A single pinhead of light that shines from the bar atop the hill.
Carry yourself to a thousand countries.
Pack your life into a dream the size of a pearl.
There are girls and treasure for all. Your wallet
cannot hold another bill. Take an interest in wildlife.
Comb the beach for the perfect shell. Lie on your back
and feel the wind with your toes. The trees rattle.
Crack your knuckles like a king.
Some leaves float to the ground as graceful as canoes
turning through a gentle stream. Others fall
and disappear like shooting stars into a crumpled universe.
A pile of leaves. Your amazement at how they fall.
A drunkenness you feel in your chest.
The wind running through your toes
and anything else you care to consider
can be done here.

SPIDER'S 3AM
for Adam

Here is the art of stopping the world with the cheapest rum
sold between this bar and the tip of Orion's sword.
Cut the palm trees out of your life, there is bad music and no girls for all.
Carry a torch through memories of concrete and rain, rats
and a landlord you buried in damp earth, her ruby smile
traded for the smoke singing up from the ashtray and into your good eye.
The taste of copper stings your tongue. You pull a molar from your mouth
and pay the bar in gold. Men call you sir and ask for work.
You lie and say yes. You lie and say no. Nothing is clear in your mind.
You've been gone too long and don't remember where you belong.
The lies eat away at your spine. The only thing you know is this bar is home.
Spider webs and camouflage draped along the walls.
A trough of a pisser that drizzles sadder than rain.
A bald man named Spider asleep behind the bar.
On the wall a calendar girl smiling at you
from another month you can no longer recall.

AT SUNSET BEACH

Carry your things to the ocean. Lay them out upon the rocks.
You have built a wall around your sentimentality
and it's cracking down the seam. You know a woman
will crumble your lies like brown sugar between her fingers.
Her eyes like blades that carve you in four.
Some women instantly have your number.
You begin like a fool until you've counted
your money and given it all away.
When the final tip of the sun slips below the horizon
the sky will flash green but you keep your eyes
on a brown woman wrapped in thin cotton and miss it altogether.
By the way she smiles you know for sure it was true,
but to each their own. Her smile quick as lightning warming you
from the memory of thunder and a colder home.
A grey house where you were banished to the cellar
to forget about love. The sky just flashed a brilliant green
and the woman will walk past you and out of your life forever.
How strange to want to love a stranger.
How strange to convince yourself that your life just passed
a turn off and kept heading north. No left turn. No sudden crash.
How strange that your favourite places point west,
that at sunset there was a green flash across the sky, a woman smiled
and your heart spun as if a drop of the sun slipped inside your chest.

SOUNDS OF NOT SLEEPING

Outside my window, more crickets than stars.
A universe dwarfed only by the howling
of the neighbour's dog.

THE LANDLORD SPEAKS OF ROSES

Three months in the jungle and you can still hear her plea for rent.
You've vacated the house and left the oven on.
One day it will burn to the ground and you'll snicker
but choke to death on guilt, gasping for forgiveness,
you've never followed through with malice.
The landlord speaks of roses and you think of returning home.
Palm leaves thatched above your favourite stone.
How it sits just out of reach from the waterfall's mist
and cradles your chest like a kiss born out of nature's
intention for a vagabond life. A waterfall is a tower
born before invention. Blue sky is a good reason to look up.
Life without love is a freedom you taste on the back of your tongue,
while the rest of your body turns to bone.
Your landlord is a tyrant who wants compensation for a condemned home.
You write a letter and drop it in the box,
There is no good reason to die of starvation.
There is no need to suffocate in an earth full of air.
Sincerely, Tenant 1998 wishing you the best of care.

CORNERED BY CONVERSATION

It's when you are mistaken for an intellectual that you feel love
for your favourite stone. You are held ransom by the memory
of your mother's request to sit up straight and finish your food.
A woman with eyes of cement kisses your cheek as you speak of wind.
Her husband sings in a thousand shades of grey but her beauty is never praised.
You swim through the night but only manage to spill your drink
and tell one bad joke. People smile at you just the same.
You drown in your own sweat. Your hair falls out.
When they pull you up by the arms your soaked muscles separate from the bone.
The woman smacks you in the face with her perfume.
It doesn't wake you but opens doors as the courtyard crumbles with shame.
Wild flowers cultivated in rows. Pristine foods crafted by the insane.
People nibbling in your mind while you drown on dry land
without even the slightest chance of rain.

ROSEAU, DOMINICA

At the bottom of the gorge, below the waterfall,
you realize your sense of beauty has been callused.
The hummingbird with opal wings nothing more
than a distraction from cynicism. The hike back
through the jungle a testament toward green.
The small town and cobblestone streets that turn silver
with rain. In your mind it becomes a question of beauty.
How when you return the cruise ship will be harbour side.
That worst time of day. Not rage or anger but an annoyance
brought on by ignorance. Yours or theirs. The shit they buy,
how for that four hours you'll be pegged as a tourist.
It'll take you five drinks to become sentimental again
and you'll quit smoking next year. If you could be bothered
you'd stand at the pier and shout them across the ocean
to an oblivion you will hopefully never know.

Tourist is a stupid word for yourself.
Somewhere back home a man is working
your job that you never had. If you think hard enough
he's married your wife, bought your dog and taken your seat
at the local hockey game. Sometimes you just wish
for a definition of home in one word.
Years will die hard but you remember the fine ones,
the places of beauty, words you expect others to know.
How you speak in local dialects and return home,
in some ways, wishing you never left. Two years since
a Christmas in the cold. Rum tastes sweetest
in the heat and you've borrowed your last few
days on bad credit. Still there is a triumph in every way of life.
Tonight you'll bunk in a hammock,
a few meters from the beach.
Tomorrow will be another day
where you choose your sins
by the wind and tide and a feeling
that you should now be moving on.

SOLOMON'S WIVES
Carla Funk

SOLOMON'S WIVES, NO. 1:
PHARAOH'S DAUGHTER

Eight days across sand our caravan traveled,
the camels' backs bundled with gifts.
The best figs and doom-palm fruit, jars of lotus
tallow, finger and toe rings newly jewelled
with ruby, lapis lazuli.

On the sixth night from Egypt, we rode
the incandescent border of a small city,
cedar groves flickering against the sky.
Gezer. I heard a servant say it.

In my lap I held the gold flask of soil,
the dowry of Gezer's rich earth.

I must explain.
I knew nothing of my father's gift
until it was too late.

The village was nearly empty, my father consoled.
Most houses deserted before the fire began,
speaking as though the fire leaped
from the sun instead of torches.
How the families must have streamed
to the sea, footprints erased in ashes.
Your husband wanted clean land, my father said.
A new city for a new wife.

We arrived at Solomon's kingdom, our camels'
hooves black with soot,
the smell of smoke in my hair.

In his palace, bath after bath
in the huge bronze basins
and I couldn't wash clean.

cont...

My throat thick with musk
the first night I breathed his skin.
His arm draped over me
while he slept, hot coals
across my breasts.

Pharaoh's daughter . . .

My husband's gift to me, my own palace
next to his and the echo of empty hallways.
This bedroom becomes more a tomb
each night, my dreams hieroglyphed
with the black bones of horses,
houses whose stones are still hot
to the touch. I wake in the dark,
blankets wrapped around me,
and my skin like that city burns.

SOLOMON'S WIVES, NO. 61:
THE SHULAMMITE

The first time you came to my father's vineyard
I hid behind a stack of baskets, embarrassed.
My dove in the clefts of the rock, in the hiding places
of the mountainside, show me your face,
let me hear your voice. With you,
three wives whose arms were ivory
next to my sun-dulled skin. Their necks ringed
with silver and sapphire. Around my own,
the wooden whistle my little brother carved
to call the dogs from the pasture.

It must have been a dream, the next time you came,
startled me as I washed my hair in a bucket of water,
your fingers wiping soapsuds from the back of my neck.
Shearing all morning in the barn, I smelled of sheep.
You untied my apron and held it to your cheek.

Come away, my lover,
and be like a gazelle . . .
on the spice-laden mountains.

I was the most difficult to take away.
My brothers hid me in the dry well
behind the chicken coop, saying
her breasts are not yet grown.

She must eat well, my mother told you,
unbruised fruit, only the softest bread.
Father insisted I have my own bedroom
in the palace, a window, my quilt
from home. Will she be warm
in the rainy season,
so close to the river?

cont...

Our wedding night in the vineyards
of En Gedi, the tent spread with flowers,
and your hands stained red
from picking henna blossoms
all morning on the limestone cliffs.

Shulammite . . .

Let my lover come into his garden
and taste its choice fruits.
Calamus, cinnamon, myrrh and aloes.
Your tongue on the tip of mine,
all the finest spices.

You begin at my forehead and move down
to my feet, every part of my body
blessed: your teeth are like a flock of sheep
coming up from the washing,
your temples behind your veil
are the halves of a pomegranate,
your waist a mound of wheat
encircled by lilies.

You are not like this with the others,
do not go to their bedrooms in the morning
with slices of cantaloupe and orange,
do not feed them, and kiss
the juice that runs down their chins.

SOLOMON'S WIVES, NO. 71: LETTERS TO ELISHAMA

The vineyards are being harvested again. The children running through the palace have purple mouths, stained tongues and fingers. All day, the servants dance in huge vats of grapes, pressing wine with their feet. At night, do they go home to lovers who kiss their dark toes? I miss you coming in from the vineyards, the back of your neck smelling like sun.

*

A new wife has moved into my room. Her black hair is long, past her ankles, and shines blue in the sunlight. She speaks a different language, words so shrill and quick she sounds like a cricket. In her sleep, she clicks her tongue against the roof of her mouth, and I pretend I am at home in bed, listening to my mother call the cats in from the dark. In his night-shirt at the kitchen table, Father eats apple cake and hums through his nose. The house smells of cinnamon, and you wait by the goat-barn for the candles to be blown out, my parents to fall asleep. You tip-toe to my window and whisper for me to come outside, the crickets are singing to the moon, the moon is dipping into the river, the river is so warm. Come, you whisper, and I do.

*

Tonight my husband found the scar, shape of a miniature bird above my left eyebrow, traced its outline with his fingers. He asked how I got it, was I born with it? And I wanted to tell the story over and over to him, say your name aloud. Elishama and I, we ran as fast as we could, the neighbour's geese chasing us all the way from the pond and I tripped on a tree root and fell into the fence, blood running down my face and we laughed and you took off your shirt and held it to the cut on my forehead and kissed me, the first time, our lips salty and throats full of our hearts, we'd run so fast.

Yes, I told him, I have worn this scar since birth.

A mark of God, Solomon tells me, a sign of the life He would have for you, flight of spirit, ascent of joy. His fingers touching the scar carve you deeper in my heart.

SOLOMON'S WIVES, NO. 213: SLIPPERS

For months, my younger sisters
brushed their sun-white hair with almond oil,
rubbed the soles of their feet with sea coral
to smooth the calluses, wrapped and re-wrapped
their slender bodies with the softest linens.

When they saw his chariots descend the mountain
they shrieked from their bedroom, waved their arms
out the window, their bracelets jangling like bells.

On the kitchen porch, Mother tucked my feet
like secrets into the new pair of slippers,
whispered he'll never notice them.
Dark evenings by candle she'd embroidered
a garden of carnelias, lapis petals, vines
curled around the heels. The threads shimmered
like stones in Father's finest goblets.

*

Before I learned to walk my feet were wrapped
in muslin, six baby toes on each pink foot
Mother hid me from the village women,
afraid of their superstitions, speculations.
A firstborn blemished is a womb's curse.
Surely she'll go lonely to her grave.

As a child, slippers every evening after bath,
sandals sewn with leather over the toes.
My barefoot sisters climbed trees
quick as weasels, laughed from the high branches
at my awkward feet struggling
against the smooth chestnut trunks.

At the river I was kept on shore
while children swam like fish melting
into the current, their muddy bodies
finning through the water.

And after, alone, I'd slip from my sandals
into water, clay oozing between each toe,
holding me there until the moon grew
and pelicans returned to the riverbank.

My father always waited at the door for me,
half-burned candle in his hand, threatening
to lead me barefoot through the village,
child of some strange god
who makes mistakes.

*

Father lined us up under the sycamore trees
for Solomon to choose. My sisters giggling,
tucked their hair behind their ears
to show new earrings, sapphires bought in the city.
He kissed their foreheads then came to me,
knelt in the dirt to everyone's surprise.
Beautiful feet, he said, his fingers tracing
the pattern of flowers, my mother's fine stitches.
As though you have grown from a garden.

*

A year after my arrival, unannounced
he entered my room.
Barefoot on the bed, I awoke with his lips
slipping over each toe, stopping at the sixth
as though he'd miscounted.

You must cover your feet, he whispers,
bringing slippers home for me
from every land he travels. Slippers
blessed by a faraway priest, slippers
sewn from white cat fur, yellow slippers
dyed in saffron, the scent of my footsteps
wherever I walk.

SOLOMON'S WIVES, NO. 647: HOMESICKNESS

I was born on water
where river dolphins splashed our boat.
Father called me Little Fish.
Before I learned to walk, I swam.
My arms became fins,
my legs, a slippery tail.

Only I could untangle Father's fishing nets
underwater, hold my breath so long
my cheeks nearly opened into gills.

Mother made my bed from a torn sail,
hung it below the window
so I could smell the river.
Every night, the soft lowing
of water yaks across the bay.

*

My cedar bed anchored
to the earth. I've not slept
long enough to dream myself
across the deserts
to where paddlefish leap along our boat
and ginkgo nuts drop from their trees
into Mother's hands.

What is the smell
of hot rice soup, bamboo boiling
over the firepit on our river shore?
What is the sound of sand ducks
breaking open the mornings
with their sharp quacks?

My eyes still shut, I feel
for the nets along the boat,
my fingers working to untangle
these knots, my hands
in the water I call home.

SEASON OF STRANGERS

Chris Hutchinson

THE NEXT POEM I WRITE

will win her back
will bid her farewell
will be lost by her
  having never been read
    then at last discovered
      after both of our deaths
will be a lie
  or such a new kind of truth
    it resembles a lie
will be my last poem
  or my first
    of many last poems to come
will be a prayer
  in the form of a plea
    or a curse
will be form
will be content
will contain form
will formalize content, that is
  its metaphors like a mother's love
    will tenderly reconcile warring twins
will not be about my mother
  ostensibly
will not use the word "ostensibly"
will not make an iota of sense
will not be written under the influence
will not admit influence
  nor influence
will not be fluid, that is flow
  but remain fixed instead
    aesthetically pure and unwordly
      convincing Plato's ghost at long last
      he was wrong
will be read only by ghosts
will be ghost-written
will be a poem about a poem
  being written and read only by ghosts
will be this very poem
will thwart paradox
will make clear sense
will do what a poem should
  and should not do
will be misquoted
will discover eloquence
  in the presence of love, god help me
    the next poem I write will remember sooner
to mention love.

VARIATION ON A THEME
for Teresa

it's the timing that's important,
the incessant, eternal music of things
like waiting for the red wine to hit
before you smoke your last cigarette,
mingling the two together
for that small but perfect ache
on an evening such as this.

a cup of tea to stay awake
since you can't sleep anyway—
only the cat is lost
in its important dreaming.
but listen: glen gould hums
off key behind his piano
as you too sing
these crude little songs
to keep the whole universe
company.

SUMMER

world-without-end
promise of blue and the sun
like the holy, singular, OM.
love
      lost, you almost relish
as the warm leaves of trees wave
like a crowd of small green saints
blessing your every deliberating
step: a dream of transcendence
as the sidewalk goes mad
with potential distances
before you stumble,
thinking of her.

this is the season of strangers
touching: a casual purity
which every moment yearns for,
when memories overlap
like the slurred words of a lamenting drunk,
this is the season of desire for desire's sake
before the conspiring multiplicity of worldly suffering
arrives with September's wind-blown leaves.
yet all this is not enough.

inside the heat of brooding
city traffic you hallucinate her
as she was, one summer ago,
ecstatic and lonely for you,
begging for experience, while you remained
fixed beyond her longing like a lone, hot star,
already consumed with your own impossible want.

one summer later, this
is the intrigue of a child
peeling back his congealed blood
to observe the terrible,
seemingly eternal
life beneath the wound.

THIRTEEN SPIDERS

1.
A spider slowly spun a web
in the corner above the end
of my bed as I lay reading
Kafka.

2.
On some days
it's best to remain
crumpled in a ball
beneath the sheets
like a spider
feigning death.

3.
My old lover would shriek
at the sight of a spider. She left me
for a man with a kinder smile.

4.
Even in suburban households
wolf spiders crawl
like nightmares from the sinks.

5.
As the Buddha found
the eight-fold path
of awakening, a spider
descended the Bodi tree
on a diamond string.

6.
The spider never sleeps
or so we think.

7.
I kept a spider
for a pet once—
his glass cage a monastic cell
and I the god
he despised.

8.
And on the eighth day
God awoke to discover
the spider, gone.

9.
O radiant skin cream angel I pray
a thousand baby spiders hatch
from your unwitting cheek.

10.
Before rain, the sky, swollen
with grey light: Somewhere
the spider must be feeding.

11.
When you wash a spider
down the drain, she's reborn
an octopus.

12.
There is a kind of spider so large
it preys on birds. There are places
where everything is magnified.

13.
The earth at the end grew feverish.
Everything held its breath.
The spider unfolded its hidden wings
and fluttered towards the sun.

THE SUN

When the sun is a presence in the room, a visitation of emotion like that too-long-absent sense of childlike equanimity; or when its warmth feels on your stiff neck like the same feeling a lover once imbued you with: a lingering erotic peace: what you once knew, or thought you knew as love; when a super-heated ball of gas millions of miles removed away in space comes-on to you in the middle of the afternoon, expect only to surrender to the day as it dances around your immobility, and your silence, a gently yearning rippling out in every direction like music, as motes of dust meander inside the matrix of leaves of the prayer-plant—leaves like hands splayed open in adoration, worshipping this mid-day light; and to each moment as it sleeps in time, a lazy transcendence, like the easy way insight comes to you after your first few drinks—everything significant and all-resembling, an infinity of metaphor . . . although it's only this room you're in, and the sun like a poem: placing every day in splendour.

COMPASSION

1.

cherry blossoms, the tiny fingers
of newborn painters, brush against
a uniform sky of white, feel
the droning ache drawn taut
above your head, its cool smoothness
like glass, frictionless detached.

2.

the purple of the blossoms,
the distance of desire, the end of love.
what name for pain that twists
you into something so unknown
as a prism twists the light
into colours you can't see?

3.

tree roots, the nocturnal tongues
of alchemists, taste the earth,
drink in its bitter soil, transforming
this darkest element into a song
of grief and luminosity to soothe
your senses back awake.

R O O M

because the room knows
it can never go outside
I bring it things I think it will like:
peels of bark from the sad arbutus,
the bones of tiny animals
who lost their tentative homes,
bits of broken beehive
and coloured glass whose hues have suffered
beautifully from many tides.

because the room and I
have only lately become acquainted
we shyly waltz together
like red and blue ink inside
the clear water of silence
or stalk the slightest sound
like two wolves, starving
around their own faltering desire.

because the room still remembers
its previous guest leaving
so suddenly without warning or farewell,
it insists I change the locks, bar the windows,
contain our mutual emptiness,
give no one a second chance.

because the room is lonely
I whisper a few words each morning
steady and soft, like the incantation
of prayer, hoping the perfect phrase
will unlock the door the room keeps
deep within itself like a secret heart;
this door I'll walk through one day
and never return.

THE NATURE OF WOMEN, SOUP AND SKY

Aubri Aleka Keleman

THE NATURE OF WOMEN,
SOUP AND SKY

The morning begins so clear and bright,
and the women who live close to the horizon
can't resist taking out their shiny scissors
and cutting large swaths of blue
out of the sky.

They stir these fresh trimmings
into their soup pots.
Bowl after bowl
is ladled out to waiting children.
Even the youngest are given
small careful spoonfuls.

The children eat the soup
and love the taste
of open space.
For a while it makes them run in wide circles.
Then they lay down, sad.
This much space
gives them growing pains.
They want to get bigger
just to fit more inside.

The women sing the children to sleep,
but they know this sound doesn't fill them,
it only quiets them.
When the children are dreaming
the women talk about other recipes.
They are planning to steal
bits of mountains, and cloud.
Tomorrow they will haul buckets of water
up from the sea.

BUTTONS

Buttons keep breasts hidden,
at each keyhole an eye
watching the fingers
that press against them.
One involuntary blink
their only expression
as clothes are set aside.

Open-eyed, buttons watch dreams
from the closet at night.
They are unmystified
by the mind's intimate movements.
They recognize themselves
in the shapes that are chosen:
a ring, a motorcycle, the wheel of fortune.

Buttons know
that the earth and the moon
have yet to be stitched in place.
They know the sun has been pressed
through a slit in the dark
to keep things together,
to hide the true skin
of the sky.

SOMEONE HAS MADE A MISTAKE: THESE WOMEN ARE FISH

Now, after long years of marriage
certain signs begin to show.
My mother bites down on words carefully,
thinks of the letters hook-like
that will catch her upper lip.

Each night my uncle winds my aunt
in the net he first used
to pull her from the sea.
He removes her scales
with a pair of tweezers,
leaves her skin soft and dull.

My grandmother has changed colour,
the blue beneath the surface
runs closer to her skin.
Even her smallest movements
are awkward and slow
without a strong tail
and agile fins.

This time before diving
I do not touch my hands to my neck
to feel the place
where skin has healed over gills.
I jump,
and wait underwater
for my first breath.

THE MOON FROM ESTONIA

"Once the moon walked the earth in the shape of a man, and learned to love the ale houses where people gathered. Increasingly distracted by earthly pleasures, the moon began to neglect his duties. Every night he rose a little later in the sky, and one night not at all. The creator soon lost his temper and insisted there be no more visits to earth."

—Folk Tales from Estonia

It is beer he dreams of
from his place in the sky,
beer and pastries dusted with sugar,
pastries so light
that after just one mouthful
someone must lean close to you
to brush crumbs from your cheek.

How the moon from Estonia loves the Earth!
How he wants to grow heavier, fatter, rounder
in the arms of a woman there.
Instead the open sky, and every night spent
gazing and guiding, listening to the stars
who never sing bawdy songs,
and even if they did could never get them right,
the music of the spheres permanently in tune.

He knows that some of us
would rather be in the heavens
than sleeping in our beds,
or dragging heavy feet
from place to place.

"If I could only visit the Earth again,"
he sighs. "I would comfort them,
whisper to the smallest, saddest child:
ale, stout, apple turnovers, big bosoms, round bottoms,
sugar on the lips of a woman."

All he can give is light, and only enough
so that, waking suddenly,
we remember where we are.

JACK THINKS OF A SECOND BEANSTALK

Although he has made them both rich,
Jack's mother still nags him.
Jack how can you go about
with holes in your pants?
You're a wealthy man
and a giant-slayer,
but no one will look up to you
if you dress like that.

Unheeding Jack continues to wear
his old muddy boots
threadbare sweater,
continues to spend most of his time
out in the garden
though nothing seems large enough now.
He longs for the giant's produce,
a row of cabbages
the size of small moons,
peonies that block out the sun.

No one in the village
suspects that Jack
is still on the lookout
for that man who sold him the beans.
He would trade whatever he was asked
for another chance to be back
above the clouds,
that far from his mother's voice,
this time chopping the beanstalk
from above,
letting his stolen garden drift free.

AFTER THE PLUM
for Brad Cran

Excited by the deep purple of the plum
firm on his erect thumb
Jack pockets the fruit,
and presses even deeper into the pie.

His mother catches sight of him,
comes wailing from the kitchen:
"Dear boy, be still, don't eat your fill,
I'm saving that . . . I tell you I'm . . . Jack,
God dammit, you never listen, I told you to stop!"

But it's too late.
Now Jack has his whole hand in the pie,
and the pie shakes so on his lap
he hardly notices his mother has spoken
without a nursery rhyme for the first time.
Jack pulls from the pie all the things
his mother hoped to keep hidden from him,
things she intended to serve once a year,
slice by thin slice.

He removes
a handful of mud, a pocket knife,
a bottle of beer, a Penthouse magazine,
and last, a heart still green and thumping.
He swallows the heart,
knows the boldness of this cadence
is a drum beat leading to war.
Jack marches out the door
to the nearest highway.

His mother calls after him:
"You'll never get anywhere.
You'll never eke out a living
without knowing table manners,
geometric reasoning,
the migratory habits of birds.

There are so many things
I meant to teach you." (And now she is crying)
"You never liked Christmas pie before.
Oh Jack!
Why couldn't you stop at the plum?"

Too far from his corner
in the cottage to hear his mother's shouting,
Jack follows a crow,
moves toward the sound of traffic,
measures the earth through the triangulation of his steps.
He is glad of his heart,
hopes the green means it will grow
large enough to take over his whole chest.
Tasting the dust of other people's cars
is as sweet as Christmas pie,
so Jack sticks out his thumb
and hitches himself a ride.

RAVEN STORIES

This is how the fairy tale begins:

A woman in the very heart of the deep dark woods
comes upon three ravens
calling from the branches
of one great oak.

They offer advice:
Do not eat the blackberries on your path.
Walk until your sandals are worn through,
then keep walking.
Share your bread with the witch you meet,
but don't breathe in her breath,
or kiss her on the lips.
Follow our advice and you are sure
to save the prince.

Here is how the fairy tale goes astray:

A woman, in the very heart of the deep dark woods
questions the wisdom of ravens.
I'm not here for a prince,
I'm already married to the butcher's brother.
I cannot resist blackberries,
my feet are too tender,
and I've already eaten my bread.
I'm here for raven stories.
My brood of babies won't sleep at night
for lack of raven stories.

The ravens only shake their feathers,
look at each other sidelong
as if they have just met.
They have been a midpoint
in magical stories for so long,
they cannot picture themselves
as a destination,
as anything children might think of
before settling down to dream.

Despite their silence
the woman stands among the ravens.
She threatens them with toneless singing,
with pie shells just right for cooking ravens,
with all five of her children.
She will bring them to this spot
let them run wild,
climb the tree,
hang from it upside down,
carve their names,
tie a rope swing.
She promises to churn butter,
scrub clothes where she stands,
even though she knows
she will be in the midst of lovers
searching for guidance.
Can you blame my little ones, she asks,
for wanting to understand
the centre of things? Your hearts?
The place where you nest,
the place between beginnings
always beginning,
and ends that always come right?

Who knows why the ravens
choose to speak at last?
All that matters to the woman is they do.
All that matters to the woman is that now
she can tell these stories to her children
and when they catch sight of ravens,
they will think of the golden life
even if it is not at hand.
They will think of the golden life
these birds lift in and out of.
And for the years that pass
when there are no woods near by,
there will be stories of ravens
in the midst of every common task.
Her children will pick up black feathers
that other people pass,
they will know another life
is somehow at hand,
they will puzzle in themselves
and find it.

RAVEN ONE

I was man-made.

Here is my recipe:

Soap shavings, spit,
candle wax, bacon fat,
a rooster's cry the morning
everyone meant to sleep,
cum from the abbess,
a mug of beer an old man
intended to drink,
two dreams you've had
but will never fully recall.

(Shall I give you a hint?
A field growing up around you,
so fast your path is gone.
You don't think of that in the dream,
it's something else that keeps you there.)

The most important ingredient is honey.
Roll everything in wild honey.
Shape and squeeze until the sky is dark.

Then throw this mixture
out the nearest window.
Darkness will streak and stain,
and caught in the stick,
break into fine dark feathers at last.

Ravens made this way
are closer kin to shadows than other birds.
I can tell you how to find
each and every path
that leads to the places
cut off from the sharp delineation of light.

RAVEN TWO

Born cross-eyed, an addled bird,
there is double everything
on this earth for me.

Sometimes it makes me lackadaisical
to have so much. Twice as many
stars, double moons.
My life has never been limited
to one level horizon.

Sometimes I don't give precise enough advice
to suit travellers that pass this way.
I'll say, Just head North. And they complain.
So what if they miss their path?
Maybe that's better.
Perhaps desperation will teach them
the secret of splitting,
let each twin self go its own way.

That's what I wait for,
I want my own double to break from me,
I want to call my raven call
on both sides of the world at once.

RAVEN THREE

Creamy with a richness
untasted by any human tongue,
my call once made cats mad
with the recollection of milk.
Even the Virgin Mary
longed to run her tongue over me,
feather by white sugary feather.
I nested on the windowsills of lovers,
but they could not bear my call
for more than two nights on end.
They wept in each other's arms
instead of making love,
certain that sweetness remained
outside the human realm.

But wisdom, life, everything stains you,
white feathers fall.
Now children chase me with sticks
and the Virgin forgives them
because I am the darkest raven of all.
I track soot,
blemish the sky, remind people
darkness is only ever
a certain number of hours away.
With a rough raven's voice
I call out the things I've learned,
some of them sad, some of them strange,
and no one thinks to weep.

WHAT LEAVES US
Ryan Knighton

for Colleen ~
Bots ~
Ryan Oct/01

NIGHT IN THE RIVERBED

Pulled by the chain
of hours, another day of dying
grey light scaled & fell
from the coast. Someone saw its
secret quicksilver,
shapely water's skin
carved into flesh.

Here you are submerged
under quilt & air
worrying the pillow,
breathing endurance
into a collapsed cotton lung,

yet hooked & drawn
to some soft animal.
Ear pressed to the wall,
it thrashes for more covers
& demands some affection

as if you'd throw your tender arm
over all that black fur,
its tooth of moon
tugging your bones,
your slightest quiver pawed
by a cold grey eye
full of fish.

BRAILLE

It is January goosebumps, it is noon-hour sand
in your sandals & sometimes, when you're four,
it's bare feet clutching barnacles
in Pender Harbour. That same year
it's your father's whiskers on your cheek
& a July heat rash on your palms. It is gravel
at 16 under balding tires & it is an eternity
of ha ha ha ha after midnight.

Once it's an itchiness from the neighbour's lawn
& maybe, having fallen that summer, it is pavement
under your chin—it is definitely the stitches
that followed & it is my recently shaved head.
It is never rubbing a fish the wrong way
& it is in the delicacy of spider's feet
you were afraid to touch. It is a late supper of brown rice
& asparagus tips on your tongue & it's any set
of particular bedtime fingertips.
Vancouver's light autumn drizzle is what it is
& it's finally pressing stars to dial God.

A MECHANICS OF VANTAGE

A doctor only measures this
symptom. The brain is paralyzed by thoughts
of nothing. Astronomy understands a hole
burned through the universe
as the vacancy of one retina.
& so this one eye, the only witness
to its devastations, wanders
like all pets &
prophets, recedes in confusions
as would a frightened dog. It is left
to lick the air
like nuclear fallout. Nothing
is exactly that
kind of murder.
& the good eye is right, diagnoses
its twin, that other brilliance
locked in a science of unlight
& revelation.

INSOMNIA
for Sharon Thesen

Have a drink & then another, preparing,
a winter breeze lifting another evening's weight
& the hem of your skirt. These are
the unnecessary theatrics—black cape,
top hat, a rabbit poised, & the trick relaxes
somewhere in the detail.

Being without direction,
today lost its mastery. But there is ritual,
a show in the air, purpose piggy-backed
like pollen. Magicians
have a drink & then another,
ready to conjure unrehearsed.
Sleep, a cold run by moonlight,
the wind up your thigh.

& on stage there is commitment.
(think of the dish and spoon running away,
a cow poised . . .)

Later, something raises the sun
& some imagination, grazed
by new light, blooms. Gravity fumbles
through the pillow for leverage
& plucks panic's face. A lonely moon
elopes. & there is still you,
still poised, performing without rabbits.

MUSIC NOTE

Imagine the girl
collapsing into her seat,
descending in scale
that #20 bus,
musty in a spittle of rain,
muggy in the summer
shining. Her expression.

She rocks in its borrowed metal frame, carried away,
& skittles, a party balloon,
windy along the gravel patches.

Legs unfold into the aisle & she
stretches bony
lyrical lines. Feet carried
in measured leather shoes.

It's a dream I have
dozing away home, waking
startled downtown.

Make the best
mistake of it all,

fetch our new favourites
from a store of hundreds.
Score second hand tunes,
this doggone day
chasing beauty in transit.

TEENAGE PRELUDES
for Jason Le Heup

Long haired boys on BMX bikes
in a vacant lot

behind any KFC. Spooky old Colonel smiles
down on them, benevolent & grand—

fatherly in his twilight, as if declaring
don't worry about your vegetables

boys, skin is the real
treat. Greasy they slip from the texture

of the world to pop
their wheelies, flip & twirl radical bodies

of chrome, extend themselves
from pedals & grips

into something else. They say it's wicked,
it's awesome. They say it's choice.

Descartes would have slowed
& parked in the drive-thru light, perhaps unreasonably

wept in a practical car
to find philosophy so fast.

With the lighting of the street
lamps, long haired boys on BMX bikes

take off, astonishing
flash of Camelot, down their avenues

vaulting meridians, leaping from
the old town gridlock. There is no formula,

no secret ingredient to protect.
They chase down wind

for their hair, for its enduring brand
of estranged mentorship.

COLOUR THEORY
for Rory (1977-99)

Look, Tracy says, it works this way. Green
is to disappear all the others. What I didn't know

& a throaty peel of "Twist and Shout"
burns through the joint.

Two Ringos two tables away, gassed & up tempo for a decade
they heard about, want custody of the myth

called a good time. But my ales vanish without a clue.
She says you'll find green is not printed but you can see it

there, in not being the other colours. But that green
on TV is different, illuminated & projected to you, in you, as its

self? Now the pool table is crawling in
my eye rolling trajectories back to him

self? My brother is a blond child
in his Mr. Turtle pool. There is no water & no way.

But I am there like the water that is not
when he begins weeping for it to fill the empty

belly of his creature, for himself
to fill some future. So I turn

that world on its back, switch channels above the bar.
I am turning on the old green hose for you.

Water in its elastic shape
of memory is workin' on out

the throat of a coiled & sleeping snake. I
know it is poison

cont...

to kill a dying past
to spring some new present to life, but for you

with love I am shaking & drowning that flicker
you are you are not.

THRILLS, CHILLS AND ASPIRIN PILLS

Billie Livingston

COAT HANGERS AND
THE IVORY SNOW BABY

Sister Mary Michael has us
marching our tartaned butts
up and down the pavement
outside Parliament.
She had time today
to make signs—mine says,
Stop The Killing
across a cut-out
of the Ivory Snow Baby.
I watch the building—
They're in there now,
gunning down babies;
blowing their little heads off
before lunch.

Sister Mary straightens
my collar, reminds me once again,
You were adopted, Teresa,
imagine if your mother'd murdered you—
cut you up and vacuumed you out . . .

I choke back
what I want to throw up
and say nothing.
She shrugs her shrivelled ovaries
and heads for the front of the line
just as a man steps out
from a stew of *Choose Choice* signs.
"Praise the Pope and
pass the coat hanger,"
he screams,
wagging a broken wire in my eyes.

The grade six class shrieks,
afraid for our faces,
until he steps back into the crowd,
leaving us to pull and chew
on those last words like toffee.

POSITIVE

In the Women's Clinic,
filling out sheets of sexual
history, I want to wrap them
round my body and head; prevent
my eyes from seeking, being sought
as I check off Methods Used:
Withdrawal.
I check it along with Condoms.
Guilty, Irresponsible—those words
slapped on like? bumperstickers.
I flick at my insolent stomach,
dreaming the usual cramps and gore.

Papers in order, I hand them
to a woman who hands me a cup
and points to the door with the
skirt-wearing stick figure
and I will my body to
pee the right hormones—Implore it,
silently chanting, Bleed, Bleed.

In the tiny mint-coloured room,
eyes sticking on the silver
stirrups on a mint-cushioned table.
My brain leaps into the green saddle,
spurs shining and gallops away,
leaving my eggs behind.
Until the return of the woman—
Pregnant slips through her lips.
Jangling onto my file, it ricochets
up off the ceiling and down into
my defiant belly, rolling over and over
until I feel the nausea I'd checked no to.

And Partner? comes next.
Business Partner? Dance Partner—
Partner in crime?
Yes. I make one up.
Because.
Because if I don't I'll cry and I'll
have to confess, admit one lousy night
with a gardener from California.
Tree planter, Sperm planter,
all the same now. And it's
too late—tears; spring rain
on fertile ground.

Oh dear, she says in her Irish lilt.
Her name tag says, Gertrude.
Only a Gertrude would say, Oh dear, now.
Abortion? follows.
Nod. Yes. Of course, I drizzle, grateful
she said the word first.
How will he feel? He?
If he were sick, would you ask how I felt?
I want to say this. To feel powerful,
to be angry. But I can't be angry with
Oh Dear Gertrude. I'm too lonely
and thankful and

besides, the rain is torrential now
down my cheeks my throat and I can't speak.
Don't worry, we'll look after you.
Gentle Irish Gertrude
looks suddenly militant,
Be grateful you live in Canada.

IN SOMEONE ELSE'S BED

I lie awake under a rumple
of cotton and feathers, feeling the weight
of his ankle crooked over mine
in an effort to touch, keep touching,
acknowledge me through the fog of his dreams.

Awake and feeling the absence
of his hunger—the perfunctory touch
of my foot in lieu of my tongue,
my breast, or the tangle of frustration
between the softest flesh of my
restless legs.

Alone and feeling her
in this room like an aspirin
slowly disintegrating in my throat.
It is still her bed, I know,
as the smell of her curls up inside
my nostrils, down my throat.
I gag. Quietly.
Don't want to wake him.

Her ghost sleeps coiled around a
picture frame that is coiled around
her, coiled around him.
In the dim light playing about the patches
of dark I almost believe I see
her underwear trailing, silken, sulking
across their vanity.

Until now, and still now, his tongue
has only found me in my bed, my
stark white room, vacant of all
scent but the musk he found in me,
void of all sound but the insistent clucks
of my white clock teasing
yanking away minutes we had left
to devour each other.

In this room, the clock is red and utters
a reserved hum so that time
hangs thickly still and I am
locked in the circumference of a second,
alone and shivering on a bed where
ardour drove their nights into mornings and
that crimson clock cried out
as if they needed to be woken.

THE THREE OF US
HERE BLINKING

Not quite midnight and streetlights are gawking
tall in my window. Somewhere
another time zone has you
just getting to dessert but
not before your touch-tone fingers rake
this tuneless jangle down my spine: bet your fingers fussed
napkin over corners between courses, wiped
themselves before folding neat, excusing to the nearest phone.

I know because I know your ring: 3 times then a blink; unending
sure blinks on my answering machine.

Mostly I feel
numb, can't
even get a good guilt-on, believing
that blink is yours, red
with grief at the sight of my bare
ass in another man's hands.
I imagine you'll say, when I tell, and I will,
that I was too busy being

the self-absorbed, self-indulgent, self-self bitch
that I am.
Or no.
You won't say that, not the B-word. You'll clear
throat, tell me it's unfortunate that I have rejected
love and security
(S.O.S. pads and babies) in favour
of fleeting and cheap
(A strange wet mouth that whispers diamond down
 my hip).

Suppose I'll humble, agree
because I won't want to say what really this is: Carnivorous—
With him I'm no Kewpie, he's not afraid
to slam me to the wall, smile
when he tells me I'm bad and, just for now, I
get to star in
every hurtin' song they ever wrote. "It's all so gauche," you'd
say, perhaps, "You picked a fine time to leave me." So I don't
bother with you now—Instead I pin
his wrists, still
him with my thighs, turn my head
from your red and change my name to Lucille.

THRILLS, CHILLS
AND ASPIRIN PILLS

      mother declares—'nother great getaway
           'nother escape
                    from the landlord/social
worker/phone company/
    lover /
        Welfare /
        Children's Aid

    Leeches, she mutters, take take take—they want my
money/freedom/body/child and we run
again   again   away

 boyfriends /
      sugar daddies /
          stray men pay for
              planes /
                  trains /
                      wine / Librium / wine /wine

      And we settle a few months
          —rest   rest

      Welfare / social workers / Children's Aid come
      to   look   through closets / cupboards / drawers
      for evidence; a man/his shoes/his shaving cream

Another new school/friend/fight
          —no riff-raff, she says
             I saw not I seen—It isn't not it ain't—just because
we're stuck in a sewer
          doesn't mean we're rats

Men and wine don't mix with neighbours
                    —a social worker announces her visit;
                    evaluation of my situation / custody
                    rabbit from hat! Mother has money for
                    a plane magic—last week we scrounged
                    in her crumb-bottom purse

'Nother great escape

—pack /
        grab/
                hurried/
                        harried we scramble into another checker taxi-cab

I HAVE THIS THING

My phone doesn't ring anymore, not the old way. It sounds
nothing like a bell now—the new phones gargle—belch when squashed
between cushions the way mine is now.

It's my mother. She says there's one other thing. And she pauses
as if the call she made two and a half minutes ago was just a ruse, a lead
in for something she remained gutless to set free before stuffing the
receiver back in its cradle like a sock in its mouth.

I've been thinking, she says. And I remember her old boyfriend,
the one who used to say, Don't think—please don't think. I hate to leave
you alone for fear you think.

I've been thinking, she says, if you should ever find me dead . . .

Uck. Must you?

Grow up, it's going to happen sometime. Just listen—and she
starts to giggle, Oh shit why did I start this.

She clears her throat in the way one might place a plush red pillow
down for the King's cat. Ok, let's say you come over and find me dead in
my bed.

Sigh. Ok. You're dead.

Well, first. You know I take out my partial plate at night and put
it beside my bed. On the night table. Right? . . . well to begin with, could
you put my teeth back in my bloody head. I can't stand the idea of them
finding me dead and toothless.

She has some kind of Marilyn Monroe Death-with-Beauty
fantasy. This is also evidenced by the eyebrows she pencils on every night
before bed, with or without company. She wants the cops to hover over
her corpse and say Oh God, why her, how can the world go on without
this lush radiance to light the dawn? She's sixty-three now.

Ok. Teeth in.

Wait. And also . . . I have this thing . . . Well ok, it's a thing. It's,
well when I was going with—ok it's a vibrator. I just don't want—If you
could just make sure that—

Oh. Got it: Teeth in /Vibrator out.

Ack! Yes. Just put it back in my drawer—No! What I mean is:
get rid of it if it's out of my drawer—Or in my drawer. The second
drawer from the top. If you could just get rid of it before anyone else
comes . . . Oh Christ, I hope it's you that finds me.

SOME GIRLS DO

Teresa McWhirter

There was a girl with pink hair who lived in the city in an apartment she shared with a cat that had never been outside. The cat liked to sit by the window and watch the traffic and when it snowed he would sit on the ledge and try to catch snowflakes through the glass. The cat also liked to drink beer.

Before the girl came to the city she lived in a small town and didn't have pink hair. She had big hair and wore tight jeans. She listened to heavy metal and hot-knifed hash on stovetops, or sat in the back of pickup trucks on lawn chairs and drank beer. The girl went cruising with her best friends. They drank coffee and complained that there was nothing to do in their small town. They stood in front of the 7-11 a lot, waiting for something to happen.

As soon as she was able, the girl left the town and went to the city. The people who left the small town achieved a small degree of fame but most stayed and worked at the mill. The girl's best friend worked as a checkout girl at the grocery store and bought a Toyota Tercel. Her other friend moved to Calgary and married a mechanic.

The girl liked living in the city and going to different bars and restaurants. She liked going to movies and coffee shops. The girl went to school and took film classes and psychology and learned about painters and Greek gods. She became a vegetarian and wrote stories and took up photography. After class the girl went to the pub and talked about Buddhism. She talked about feminism and Sartre. The girl liked knowing about existentialism and even though it didn't have much use for her she was glad she knew what it meant.

On holidays the girl went home to visit her parents but she found their lives a mystery, and to some degree distasteful. Her father liked to hunt and catch fish that her mother would clean and cook for dinner. He thought the girl should be married and keep house. Her mother kept a clean house and even ironed her father's handkerchiefs.

The girl and her mother went shopping together. Her mother bought her socks and underwear and wanted to hear about the boys the girl liked. The girl didn't have much to say. There were never any boys she particularly liked, and if she did they weren't around long.

The girl and her father rarely talked. Her father liked to make things in his workshop. He built her a set of shelves for her books. He sanded her dresser, removed the chipped white paint and added a coat of varnish. Her father took her combat boots to his workshop and weatherproofed them. The girl didn't like how they smelled and they were too shiny, but they kept her feet dry.

Every year when the girl came home her parents seemed a little bit older. Her mother cut her long hair and it became shorter and greyer each visit. She noticed wrinkles on her father's forehead and teased him about the hair that sprouted from his ears. Her father began to go a little deaf and watched the t.v. with the volume full blast. This annoyed the girl and by the end of the week she was glad to go back to the city.

One day the girl got a phone call from her mother. It was fall and the girl wasn't scheduled to come home for many weeks. "Your father is not well," she said, "and if you can, maybe you should come home." Her mother insisted the girl only come if she could. She said she did not want the girl to miss any classes or the cat to go hungry.

When the girl got home her father was in bed. He had lost a lot of weight and didn't go to the workshop anymore. He stayed in bed and did crossword puzzles and read books about CIA agents and government conspiracies. The girl and her mother watched movies, but the volume on the t.v. was now low so her mother could listen to her father's movements. Sometimes he would cry out and her mother would get a syringe and bottle from the fridge and go into the bedroom to give her father an injection of morphine. Then her father would be quiet for the rest of the night. In the morning the girl would go to see her father. "How are you doing?" she would ask. "I'm fine," he always answered. Then he would wink. She liked it when he winked. It was like he was playing a trick on her.

The girl called her friends back in the city. They told her about parties and nightclubs, said she should have been there. They sent postcards and letters that said the cat was doing fine and getting fat. The cat missed her, and wanted to know when she was coming back.

One day an ambulance came to take her father to the hospital. The girl and her mother moved the bookcase from the hallway to clear a path so the stretcher could go right into the bedroom. The ambulance driver picked up her father and she saw his legs were very thin. His blue pajamas hung from his hips. She got an extra blanket from the hall closet so he would not get cold in the ambulance. When they wheeled her father out the door he winked but the girl did not think the trick was funny anymore.

The girl did not like to visit her father in the hospital. She did not like the green walls and the smell of antiseptic and urine or the nurses who came in to adjust pillows. The girl did not like the feeding tubes and the bags hanging underneath her father's bed or how he became thinner and his hair fell out. He still did his crossword puzzles but now he couldn't finish them. The girl tried to finish them when her father dozed off, but she never could get many of those answers.

The girl sat with her father one day while her mother was in the cafeteria. She thought her father was sleeping and began to read her book about a town by the Wawanash river. Everyone in the town had a tragic past. It was a good book. Suddenly her father reached out his hand. The girl was startled. "What do you think about this?" he asked. "About what?" the girl said, even though she knew what he was asking. "What do YOU think about this?" she said and her father closed his eyes again.

One day her father moved into a family room that had a couch and a television. The girl was in the room with her mother one night when her father whimpered. She turned on the television so she could not hear him.

The girl went outside and smoked a cigarette. She smoked another and another. Finally she went back inside. She saw two nurses go into her father's room. The girl walked down the hallway slowly. When she opened the door the curtain around her father's bed was closed. Her mother sat in the chair crying. "Your father is gone," she said and she hugged the girl. "Do you want to say goodbye to daddy?" she asked but the girl had never called her father daddy, and she did not want to open the curtain.

The girl ran out of the room and down the hall, past the nurse's station, down the stairs and outside. She sat down on a bench and cried, and while she did she looked up at the sky. She stayed there until her mother came, finally, to get her.

The girl's brother flew home. He was very tall and suntanned. They had not seen each other in a long time. Her brother cried when he hugged her. After that he began to make arrangements. He called the funeral home and the insurance company. Her mother made sandwiches and meat trays, arranged pickles and cheeses on platters. Soon relatives began to come. The girl did not want to see them. She had not seen them since she left the for the city.

The girl had many uncles and some of them looked like her father. They smelled like tobacco and whiskey and one had a cane while another wore a polyester shirt with the buttons open. They didn't talk very much and sat quietly. They didn't say anything about her pink hair. They said she had grown up into a nice young lady.

The girl did not like her aunts much. They clucked and fussed around the kitchen. They pulled her mother around and whispered when the girl entered the room. "It's a shame, a shame," they said. They watched her mother with black bird eyes. "What will you ever do," they asked. Her mother passed them a tray and they picked at crackers.

"What have you done to your hair!" one aunt said to the girl. Her aunt had tightly curled hair a slight shade of blue. The girl wanted to ask her the same thing. Another aunt wanted to know about the classes at university but the girl didn't speak. She did not want to talk about the city or her friends. She didn't want to talk about her father. The girl sat with her brother and drank whiskey.

After everyone left her mother took a sleeping pill and her brother passed out from the whiskey. The girl went down to the workshop. It smelled of varnish and sawdust. The girl began talking to her father. She told him about her apartment in the city, and the cat who drank beer. She told him about the boy who broke her heart and the pub she liked to sit in after class. She told him everything she knew about French painters. She told her father that the boots he weatherproofed kept her feet exceptionally dry in the rainy city. She asked him why he liked to fish so much. She told her father she liked the bookshelf he made for her, and only kept her very special books on it. The girl thought maybe her father didn't know that, and wondered why she had never told him.

IN VANCOUVER, WITH JAMES

It's raining, it's Vancouver, you're waiting for James to call. You water the plants so often they die.

"He's like every other guy," Jezebel says. "It's all about the chase." You are in her studio and watch as she meticulously cleans her brushes. Jezebel is a painter who has never understood loneliness. She will not accept blame for introducing you to James, the friend of a friend of a friend. He was impressed with your varied drug connections. You have spent a lot of time in this city.

James will always get up to dance, is the one who wants the eight ball delivered. He believes in never admitting the truth, getting drunk before dinner, and will wait in the car until you get to the door. James has moments of uncharacteristic chivalry, quietly bred manners and the indolence of abandoned rich boys by which you are frequently dazzled. He keeps calling a girl who won't phone back, and that makes him like her even more.

He meets you and Jezebel at the bar where you've been drinking three hours already. Crosses his legs and leans back in his chair to study you like an exotic, red-faced bird. You concentrate on the rock band, four long-haired men pounding their instruments.

"You're a smart girl," James says. "Why are you so resigned to this life?" The singer lets out a howl. You suffer quietly.

You wish him twisted limbs. You wish him a stutter, an angry red scar, but still you marvel that he is the son of a pianist, admire the elegant curve of his chin. James collects perfect, dull blondes like coloured rocks from a lake. He studies Philosophy and speaks French, hates the cold, the rain, his endless packs of cigarettes. James cannot cook or sew or make flowers grow but his long slim fingers are heaven in your room.

James will always break your heart and dully you understand this is most of his appeal. So often you have sat drunk in his apartment, smiling dumbly as he sprawled like a sultan, the broken love seat a divan. He makes you feel like a twisted Odalisque. This is why you agree to these dim scenes and half truths; you can only dance the blues. You sleep together like shy, cold children. Slowly you forget to breathe.

You can reign for days, distant and remote. James will phone and say, I've missed you terribly. He says, you don't love me anymore and the words slip at the edge of your mouth. All it takes is the soft cinnamon walls of your apartment and Nina Simone to remember how it feels when he bends down to hear what you say. You are a small, dark girl and it makes everything seem like a secret.

You hold the phone away from your ear and from the window watch a dreadlocked girl, a small Asian man running with a shopping bag. Muslim women in flowing cloth, erupting teenage girls. A purple-haired boy waves from the corner. All this can exist around you so simply. You would explain to James how you fear the years will slip past, but it would be lost in your translation.

SQUALOUR AND BLISS:
PUNKASSES IN BAR X

A night of empty beds and bottles. Punkass needed to get laid, so there we were in Bar X. The same scene, same deluded slobs, same horny mini-men. Chin scruff, chin scruff, a siege of facial hair and oversexed hippie men who long ago lost track of their belly piercing. The bar was full of pop tarts and disco biscuits, men with big teeth and too much tongue, men who slobbered in their beers, greasy beasties who gobbled the girls with their x-ray eyes and porn manifesto. I needed to make a withdrawal from the chemical bank; the Hungarian beer was getting me nowhere.

A table of pink businessmen sat debating penis implants on cell phones. "Have some of this coke!" one of them squealed. "It'll make you feel like a million bucks!" and I said "but I don't want to feel like a big greasy pile of money." So much for the revolution. Which way to the riot, man!

Punkass was in the corner, watching mall girls in their big-haired glory sprayed stiff to the sky, motivated by their fear of oral sex and nipple hair. "Watch it, cookie!" I growled and pushed a lycra encased Jimmy Dean sausage ass outta my way. Cookie ran off to do the bump and grind, plying her breasts for an Island Lager. "Why'd you do that?" Punkass said. "She was rea-lly pretty."

I wondered how my cat Pablo was doing. That morning we shared our first hangover. Fetus Boy had been over the night before, feeding the kitty capfuls of the big beer. "Goddamn it Fetus Boy!" I had shrieked. "His brain is the size of a walnut!" It disturbed me that I was becoming the kind of person who talked about their pets to strangers.

It all came back: big white shoes and shiftless winks, Coco the butcher and slim, greedy fingers. Punkass sat perched like a peanut at a hemorrhoid convention. Oliver came up in his white afro, moaning lost love and latex. "Go back to the pokey, Joe!" I said. He's had more hands up his ass than a muppet. I worried about my shrinking limbs and diminishing pack of cigarettes.

"Didn't I see you at Sunfest little sister?" a stinking hippie asked. I can't help my dreads, man, I'm so fucking punkass I woke up one day and my tufts had turned solid. Let the slutty days of art whores reign but I've had it with weed fiends, paranoid lifeless pods who sit on your couch for hours, interminable with dullness then finally raiding your cupboards for cheesy snacks.

Punkass sat wistfully watching Christmas lights, still waiting for a girl to smile, for someone to take home and feed capers, wash her feet in jello, learn to love her dog. Then he'd watch her wring the tears from her cashmere, crying in her crantini. I saw Fetus Boy in all his Slayer loving, thrash rat glory and felt all the old feelings. "You houseplant!" I screamed, playing it cool.

I felt like crying but goddamn cheap eyeliner and hopeless bliss so I raised my beer and drank, I drank to all the Punkasses in their vitamin deficient glory, to bald death boys and their chains, to finger fuck punks, faded blondes in barrettes, bands that document their baldness.

"Punkass, I'm OUTTA here!" I'd buy a bottle of cheap wine and share it with Pablo, get fried with the feline. Carrotgirl staggered over. "I'm a magical forest creature," she said, dropping sequins and buttons like charms. The thought that an angel could burn so bright shattered all the illusions of beer and blue lights. And suddenly it was all okay, fuck the city sickness, rock whores, bar stars, death by osmosis. I decided to go back to my pink room where mushrooms bloom like madness. I was alive, six foot five and somebody could love me.

SOMETIMES GAY
MEANS HAPPY

Billeh Nickerson

Colleen,
it's always a pleasure, babe.

Stay sexy,

Billeh

BEING A FAGGOT

Being a faggot means you can wear
the tightest underwear, bathe
in the hottest hot tubs
without having to worry
about sperm counts.

Being a faggot means you can laugh
at divorce rates, the couple
on top of wedding cakes;
being a faggot means
you're a perpetual best man.

Being a faggot means you get to
hear about everyone else's
faggot friends and sometimes
their faggot uncles.

Being a faggot means you can drink
homo milk without getting embarrassed.

Being a faggot means you get invited to
baby showers, lesbian potlucks—or
lesbian potluck baby showers where
you're the donating father.

Being a faggot means you pay
into the policy
without extending the benefits.

Being a faggot means
your blood isn't good enough.

Being a faggot means
you'll still fall in love
with straight men.

LOUISVILLE SLUGGER

Think baseball he tells me
but it's difficult
on hands and knees—
the way I'd play
horseback riding
when my sister was five
& I was nine.
Think baseball and I knew
it would come down to this,
a day when I let this happen,
but I never thought I'd be
thinking baseball,
my uncles during the World Series,
my stiff leather mitt,
my grade eight gym class when
even the teacher laughed
because I threw
like a girl.

IT'S HARD TO SAY NO

When he kisses with his eyes closed,
when he calls you his Greek god,
when he lets you cheat at Scrabble,
when he reminds you of an ex,
when he smells like vanilla,
when he pets your cat,
when he breathes,
when he blinks,
when he hums while shaving,
when he makes banana pancakes,
when he fingers his nipples,
when he trims your hair—just a little,
when he talks like Donald Duck,
when he sucks on your chin,
when he tickles,
when he nibbles,
when he washes the windows,
when he knows the names of all seven dwarves,
when he burns the waffles,
when he pulls your leg,
when he eats your sins,
when he swallows
                    your pain.

IN THE SHOWER

My lover feeds me mango
with his switchblade
close against my lips.
This is when my tongue
glides easiest,
licks strings of fruit
off our skin,
into my mouth.

I want to tell him—
warm water trickling
down our backs,
my thumbs circling
his nipples—
I'm afraid the blade
might slip

but there's so much
being said right now
as he thrusts the fruit
against my stomach,
guts it
like a small animal.

DRIVING IN ADAM'S JEEP

I keep praying for red lights,
the hum of his transmission
when his hand gears down,
almost touches my knee.
Seat belts aren't the only form
of restraint.
On nights like this—
the wet asphalt making me
lick my lips—
I want him to kiss me
with the windshield wipers on.

\\Kiss me//

\\Kiss me//

\\Kiss me//

IF YOU FIT ALL YOUR LOVERS IN AN AIRPLANE WHAT KIND OF AIRPLANE WOULD IT BE?

In my dreams it's a 747 filled
with sports teams,
baseball, football, soccer—
anything with balls basically.
I'm the Captain of course,
which means I just stick it in
automatic, head back
into the cabin to take
frequent flyer applications
in the rear.

One day it could be a 737
with enough seats
for each of my lovers
to hold one of Disney's
101 Dalmatians.
At first, I'd name each pup
after the lap they sit on
but then there'd be so many Jasons
and Chrises
and Mikes
that I'd just refer to them by number.

Right now I'd need a turboprop commuter,
one of those short haul affairs
with thirty seats and a flight attendant
who gives you his phone number
if you're lucky,
honey roasted peanuts
if you're not.

How strange it seems
I once started off
in a twinseater,
no carry-on baggage,
just me and the pilot exploring
the various landscapes until
our single-engine sputters
and I realize I can never fly
in such a small plane again.

NADINE'S BRASS BED

For years Nadine's brass bed
moved around our building
like a cat
always finding itself a new home
as tenants backpacked Europe,
taught English in the East,
or, simply, started anew.

It was always someone else's turn
to make it their own, break it down
in one apartment so
it could be rebuilt in another,
the shine of its finish
reflecting around the room
as we washed our hands of
the greenish hue
one more time.

I've often wondered how many of us
have experienced its squeak,
the way it amplifies your passion
without apology,
announces it to the world
whether you want it to or not.

How different to make love
on something so full of history
instead of the futons our parents bought
or the old foamy mattresses
left over from our youth.

To make love on Nadine's brass bed
was to make love to ritual,
your fists grasped so tight
around its bars,
when you finally let go
you could see yourself
from above.

WHY I LOVE WAYNE GRETZKY—
AN EROTIC FANTASY

Because he knows what to do with pucks,
slapshots, wristshots, all that intricate stickwork
as he slips through defense men,
shoots between the legs
& scores.

Because he likes to pretend
I'm the zamboni & he
the filthy ice.

Because even if he's tired
he'll perk up
whenever I sing O Canada.

Because sometimes my dyslexia makes me see
a giant sixty-nine on his back.

Because he's always ready for overtime—
because he never shoots then snores.

Because he understands the importance of
a good organ player.

Because he calls me his stick boy.

Because he likes to be tied-up
with the laces from his skates.

Because behind every great man
it feels good.

EATING DIRT
Karen Solie

DEAR HEART

Rustbucket, little four-popper.
I've seen more of the surface of Mars

than of you, ultrasound shadow.
How you lay me low! Size of a fist

and the rest of me a fat glass jaw.

I get reports through the wire of veins,
your rabbit punches, four left feet.

I log each personal best and sleep
like a swan with an ear to my chest.

You are the first thing I ever built,

drafty and cold despite blood's small suns.
Your joinery came out all wrong.

Sweetmeat, my ugly hero, the fault
is mine. I recline and recline.

There was no time, is no time but yours.
What leisure you afford, what luxury.

HANGOVER

Yesterday left wanting, night fell
a blank. I edged
toward you at the old hotel
padded with disaster movie extras
going down with their ships.
The brain floods easily,
that old engine. Later
is a lullaby of rain scraping paint
from the streets. Show me again
how to take you home.

I have a mouth full of gasoline,
what was I saying? Something
about birds needling through trees,
the year's first wasps drilling
in the eaves. Last night,
as plants poisoned the air
under the moon, I sold you
a possibility of days on the Oregon coast
perfect as swift eggs, insinuated
Tennessee in a wet reverb,
Nashville slapback, read your palm
tracing fragrant mesquite trails
arching into purple arroyos
of the Sangre de Cristos.

Now, the day is explicit.
Swallows fall in shrieks,
from great heights. My head
is a drawer full of spoons.
No Faulkner heroine this afternoon
with flowered housedress, bourbon,
no Southern belle. My accent
makes Lutheran hymns
from what we've said of spring,
its drug-white sea and sky, horizon
briefly gone, rethought,
and the wind full of blooms.

LAST WALTZ

Shot through
with a long Montana curve
of white crosses we drop,

clay pigeons from an amphetamine sky,
hit the Poodle Dog Lounge at twilight,
beer warm and green as grass.

The owner compensates for happy hour
by hating us, his coke-fed moon face
oscillating like a fan

as our bar tabs lengthen into parables
and the sun, overcome, lurches to the west,
the day a blue ruin.

I'm tired of this, you say,
meaning me. I catch your eye as would
a strange floater in a weedy derelict lake.

For weeks you have been gazing
down the snow-eater's green throat,
to the clean young skin of a Pacific city,

in your sleep whispering
the names of grocery stores
that might provide perfect boxes

for the plates while I ride
the bed like a barge into the afternoon,
cursing your adulterous list of things to do,

your deliberate hand in its rings
writing all the ways you can think of
to tell me to take care.

BOYFRIEND'S CAR

Black Nova. Jacked up. Fast.
Rhetorical question. Naturally,
a girl would choose
the adult conspiracy
of smoked glass, darkened interiors.
Privacy, its language
of moving parts, belts,
and unfamiliar fluids.

Hot. Mean. The words
he used for it.
She added a woman's touch.
The back seat shone
like a living skin. Oxblood.
Hair in the door handle,
white white arms
pretty against
the grain, the red.

She joined the club,
difference the code
that made it real
(how does it feel?)

A word muttered snidely
by tattletale skin.
Privacy. Bruises
smuggled like cigarettes
under her clothes.
A grown-up walk,
The responsibility not to speak
a certain silly thought.

When she asked
to go home he said

Well now that depends
on you.

I LIKE YOU

You name garden pests in order
to better identify the dead.
The diazinon has taken care
of the Johnsons, you said,
coming in from the yard,
and made me a salad without
washing your hands.
It's no wonder I feel weak.
And my medicine is three days gone.
I could never keep a thing
from you. Sometimes it's better
not to speak. Your sentences
are ghastly henhouses, each word
a plank. After every lunch
I must be quarantined. But you come
and hold your hand to mine
against the glass. You are a friend,
I think, even though
my hysterical math can't discern
your sevens from your nines,
and we disagree on the function
of a denouement. You said,
only a coward reads the back page first.
Or was that me, dear,
I forget.

LOVE POEM FOR
A PRIVATE DICK

Sucker punch, true romance.
15 years reading your name
on the door, filing my nails down hard,
managing a parade of dames
whose rich husbands tire easily,
who pull Houdinis south
with proceeds of a double cross
leaving you with only style left to burn.
A currency of pain. Poor thing.
Eyes of a neglected pet
above the glass.
Who possibly can understand
what martyrs do when falling for it.

Things have gone too far for you
to admit the boredom of waking
once again to stupid noises of thirst
the dullness of a room,
a sink, a walk downtown,
the effort to reclaim
from pretty flush of evening light
a more complex drama of sunset
glaring then bloody then black,
remembering Mickey's, the White Orchid,
pinballing cops and thugs, your name
a bad itch in a good suit
you kept them coming back to scratch.
Now they snap their fingers in your face.
You track teenage Connecticut runaways
to grimy dance-halls for a fin
when I could be snug as a fifty
against your ribs.

Your name, bone fantasy
of my common desire, my eternal walk
down the peeling hall,
heartfelt tragedy at the door,
one hand on the frame
as if to test for fire inside.
What a lovely rush, lingering there
about to try the lock, on the verge,
blushing with sweet star-crossed nerve.
I've seen no pay in months, but shine
your shotgunned shoes, go out
for Ballantyne's at noon, or Cuervo
when the day is warm
and you're thinking blackly of Mazatlan.

When all is spent in plain view
what is left?
Humiliation of the overdressed
made up to kill
and always at the wrong event.

IN PASSING

Night-blind through Roger's Pass,
engine popping like a rabbit gun
after nervy ambush of tunnels.
I brake for tinfoil, bottles,
dead stares of twisted deer.
This moon-shot boneyard
is a seam of eyes.
Immigrant rail crews lost
in the slides of March
a century ago. Two Japanese dug out
clasped in each other's arms,
a Norwegian frozen in the act
of filling his pipe. No time
even to bruise.
Hidamo. Wafilsewki. Mitsumi. Sodiatis. Sanquist.
Bronze and marble statues
for the meat ride to Glacier Station.
And the whores who died cold,
full of holes, in clapboard
Columbia or the pockmarked
skin village of Golden.
A drunken doctor drowned
in a puddle of horse piss.
Years later, slide shooters
and dozers shoved 92 miles of highway
through the Selkirks' seismic muscle,
and now my four seizing cylinders
whine for a tail wind
to Saskatchewan. I Go All The Way,
Number One croons over
archival mutterings caught in the black throat
of the old Connaught Tunnel,
buried at the Summit. Accordian ballads
of accidents that wait to happen
in the rock face, snow
fall, concentrated gravity of the gorge.
My odometer books odds of sleep
in hands and head. The cat knows it,
moving through luggage in the back seat
throwing sparks.

EATING DIRT

The elongated shadow suggests
my mother. To the left
a possibility of raspberries.
In the centre of the frame
I have caught the sun full on
in bonnet and dainty shoes,
huge and white on the just-turned plot,
an early grinning vegetable
sprung up overnight feeding
methodically, in fistfuls.

Greedy rhizome, I send shoots
to gorge on portions of the yard;
there I am on the step, in the lane,
under the clothesline,
and growing larger all the time.
I wonder at the wisdom
of this documentary, its complicity
in my vice, where it has led.
After all,
some cravings are only charming
when you're small.

I've since learned,
when potting houseplants,
to lick my fingers
in private.

A TREATISE ON THE EVILS OF MODERN HOMEOPATHIC MEDICINES

"What if the vitamin makes my body stop making its own vitamins?"
Mark Anthony Jarman, "Uranium City Rollers"

"...homeopathy is based on the theory that 'like cures like'"
Oxford English Reference Dictionary

Four Tylenol with that last sweet shot.
Morning comes, you'll be a prince
on the phones, greasing wheels, making it go
with a clear head. Your guts will come around.
Little quinine at coffee. Cuts the shakes.
Sudden liver failure? Forget about it.
Cellphone tumours? Bullshit.
Look at me. 40 years and still a whip,
slick, the ticket, hyperspace.
I smoked my first cigarette at 9.
You don't know who to trust? Then don't.
Trust technology. It wouldn't send
machinery to Mars then seed
your little brain to polyps, plant
cancer mushrooms in your balls.
It can keep your dick hard all night.
What more do you need? Someone tries
to sell you blue-green algae. Fuck him.
It's a scheme. Vitamin C? Eat an orange
for Chrissakes. Send that joker back
to the co-op, to his hypocrite cronies
drumming in the woods reading Bly by night,
Rand by day. That'll soften your brain
faster than any happy hour. Do you think
no one is making money from this?
That it comes from the goodness of a heart?
Nothing comes from the goodness of a heart.
Everyone is out to fill their hole.
Like God said on the seventh day, kicking back,
feeling fine. Pick your poison,
children, leave me mine.

CHAOS THEORY

"That one body may act upon another at a distance through a vacuum
without the mediation of anything else . . . is to me so great an absurdity,
that I believe no man, who has in philosophical matters a competent faculty for thinking,
can ever fall into."— *Sir Isaac Newton*

Before this country of seminars,
its paranoid GNP a flat-earth theory
of love affairs, I lay
in leafy grove of windbreak
gated by lilac, redolent,
with ants in my hair,
and considered the bodies of men,
gravity of collarbone and hip.
Amid the plushness of bees you could say
I considered you, even then hiding
from a convergence of lovers
in the pool halls of the midwest. Sometime,
I may recall a brightness to that day,
though I suppose the sky divulged
the usual tyrant kingbirds and flycatchers
jolting through standard variants of blue.
I don't believe in fate, but did then,
having already drowned the kitten
in the rainbarrel. I cannot speak
to most of what you have done.

Air and chaos, inseparable,
the Orphics taught, come forth
from sad old Chronus, personification of time
caught in cosmogony's net. Scientists
have the space between sun and earth soaked
in forces that touch bodies simultaneously
and intimately as water, explain
the unconscious voodoo of an eye,
a look hitched north riding a pilot wave
through the overbuilt world
to prick me without ceremony,
indolent beneath centenary ash. I woke

cont...

to an intolerable reality of Patsy Montana
yodeling for her lost cowboy
through dishcloths greying in the open window,
red-eyed leghorns pecking the yard
to dust around me, the wind-up toy
of innocence finally winding down.

I could grow plump as a finch
among ineluctable branches warm as arms
believing I had always lived
with a phantom hand around my heart.
How can we drop buckets racketing
down the void of a dry well and draw
God or love like cool fresh water when panic
is a wire singing in air?
We met, that's all.
If coincidence has a law
it is lonely.

CONTRIBUTOR'S NOTES

Lori Maleea Acker was born on Vancouver Island. She has lived on and off the water in Canada and Mexico. She has a BFA from the University of Victoria and has been published in *Geist* and *The Fiddlehead*. She is currently working on manuscripts of both poetry and prose.

"Her Own Ritual" previously appeared in *Geist*. "Mechanic" and "With My Father Now And Then" previously appeared in *The Fiddlehead*. Part of this selection first appeared in the chapbook *Her Own Rituals* (Smoking Lung Press, 1997).

Shane Book was awarded the 1998 New York Times Fellowship in Poetry at NYU. This year he received the *Malahat Review* Long Poem Prize, the Charles Johnson Award in Poetry from Southern Illinois University and the San Francisco Poetry Center's Rella Lossy Award and was the recipient of a scholarship to attend the Breadloaf Writers' Conference in Vermont. He splits his time between Ottawa and New York City.

"Dust" won the *Malahat Review* 1999 Long Poem Prize. "Fall," first appeared in the chapbook, *Forgetting The Rest Beyond Blue* (Smoking Lung Press, 1997), the "Blue Journal" poems are excerpted from a much longer cycle. The form is loosely modelled on Charles Wright's series, "Tattoos."

Adam Chiles has published poems in *Vintage '95* and *'96*, *The Malahat Review*, and has work forthcoming in *Fiddlehead*.

"Almost Blue" first appeared in *Washington Square*. "Cathedral" first appeared in *Vintage '95*. "Stair" first appeared in Vintage *'96*. Part of this selection first appeared in the chapbook *Just In From Fun City* (Smoking Lung Press, 1997).

Brad Cran is a contributing editor at *Geist* magazine and publisher of Smoking Lung Press.

"Abandonment" starts with a line from Patrick Lane and appeared in *sub-TERRAIN*. "Roseau, Dominica" appeared in *Geist*. "Death of a Friend by Overdose," "Hitching," and "Imperfection" were first published in the Chapbook *Songs I Use to Chase Rye*. The remainder of the poems are forthcoming in *Stillborn at the Cornerhouse Cafe*.

Carla Funk lives in Victoria with her husband and daughter, where she writes and teaches part-time. Her poems have appeared in the anthology *Breathing Fire* edited by Patrick Lane and Lorna Crozier, in literary journals and in the chapbook *Solomon's Wives* (Smoking Lung). Her first book of poetry, *Blessing the Bones into Light*, is published by *Coteau Books*.

These poems have previously been published as part of the chapbook *Solomon's Wives*. They will also appear in *Blessing the Bones into Light* published by Coteau Books.

Chris Hutchinson sells fish and chips on a pier which is connected to the garden city of Victoria. He is currently finishing his first book of poetry.

"Room" appeared in Grain.

Aubri Aleka Keleman is a recent graduate from the University of Victoria Writing program. She is presently studying to become a childrens' librarian in Bellingham Washington. She lives in a tree top apartment with her 16-year-old deaf cat "Snuggles" whom she did not name. She was first published by Smoking Lung Press in '97.

Ryan Knighton was born in Langley, BC during the formative 1970s. He is a co-founding editor of *Tads* and editor of *The Capilano Review*. In East Vancouver, where he makes his home, passers-by often find his blindness worthy of praise, comment or scrutiny.

"Night In The Riverbed" appeared in *Prairie Fire*. "Braille" appeared in *The Malahat Review*. "A Mechanics Of Vantage" appeared in *The Capilano Review*. "Insomnia" appeared in *Descant*.

Billie Livingston's first novel, *Going Down Swinging,* will be published by Random House Canada in January 2000. She lives in Tsawwassen with a stuntman and a cat.

"Coat Hangers and the Ivory Snow Baby" appeared in *The Antigonish Review*. "Positive" appeared in *TickleAce* and *The Home Planet News* (U.S.). "In Someone Else's Bed" appeared in *Contemporary Verse 2* and *Bystander* (Australia). "Thrills, Chills and Aspirin Pills" appeared in *PRISM International*. "I Have This Thing" appeared in *The New Quarterly*.

Teresa McWhirter's contributions to the arts include publications in *Sassy, Bust, filling station* and the smoking of Du Maurier cigarettes. She has just completed her first novel and is currently at work on a collection of short stories.

"Her Father Liked To Fish" and "Squalour And Bliss: Punkasses In Bar X" appeared in the chapbook *Some Girls Do* (Smoking Lung Press, 1998)

Billeh Nickerson's column, "Hardcore Homo," appears monthly in *Xtra! West: Vancouver's Gay and Lesbian Bi-weekly*. He is a contributing editor to *Geist* magazine. His first book of poetry, *The Asthmatic Glassblower and Other Poems*, will be published by Arsenal Pulp Press in the fall of 2000.

"Being a Faggot" appeared in an online version of *The Church-Wellesley Review*. "Louisville Slugger" and "In the Shower" appeared in *PRISM International*. "If You Fit All Your Lovers On an Airplane What Kind of Airplane Would It Be?" and "Why I Love Wayne Gretzky—An Erotic Fantasy" appeared in the *Church-Wellesley Review*.

Karen Solie is from southwest Saskatchewan and has lived in Victoria since 1993. She has recently published poetry in *PRISM International, ARC, Event, Wascana Review, Indiana Review*, and *The Malahat Review*. Her work is included in the anthology *Breathing Fire* (Harbour, 1995). Her chapbook, *Eating Dirt*, was published by Smoking Lung Press in 1998. She is currently writing her doctoral dissertation in English at the University of Victoria.

"Last Waltz" and "Boyfriend's Car" appeared in *Wascana Review*. "I Like You" appeared in *PRISM International*.

ACKNOWLEDGMENTS

A special thank you to Brian Lam and Blaine Kyllo at Arsenal Pulp Press and to Alma Lee and Dawn Brennan at the Vancouver International Writers Festival. This book would not have been possible without their support, encouragement and hard work.

As well a special thank you to co-founders Barclay Brick Blair and Shane Book for their work, creativity and dedication during the first two years of Smoking Lung.

And for their support over the last three years, Smoking Lung Press thanks: Debra Miller, Jenny Durrant, Andrew Musgrave, Mike Lane, Kerri Embry, Lyle Neff, Brian Hendricks, Patrick Lane, Lorna Crozier, Susan Musgrave, Stephen Hume, Stephen Osborne, Patty Osborne, Barbara Zatyko, Mary Schendlinger, Mellisa Edwards, Robert Ballantyne, Brian Kaufman, Mark Jarman, Carmen Derkson, Sarah Hill, Lana "Smoking Bouquet" Hill, Leanne Nash, Open Space, The Western Front, Chuck's Pub, The Billy Bishop Legion, The Impresario, The Cornerhouse Cafe, Linda Cran, Bruce Cran, Murray Madryga, Kathy Jack, Alexandra Lechenko, Chad Pawson, Carol Hamshaw, Marianne Corless, John Lucas, Rosanne Harvey, Leslie Neilson, Venus, High Haired Jerome, Jeremy McCarron, Matt McCarron, Robin "take it from the top" Steen, Brad Ellis, Laird Salton, Blair McGarvey, Jason Buzza, Nicola Gubbins, Graeme Hamilton, John Roe, Mike Murrin, Rashid Hille, Ryder Bryan, Jason Bryan, Jennifer Lovegrove, Hal Niedzviecki, Diane Kadota, Dan "The Superfan" Hopkins, Brad Bentz, Yasmeen Strang, The Vancouver International Writers Festival, The Canada Council for the Arts, Sue Stewart, Hillside Printing, Native Images Tattoo, Jeremy Glenn, Carly Louth, Ryan Klaschinsky, Erica Gosjich, Mandelbrot, Craig Saunders, *Canadian Forum*, Anvil Press, Coteau Books, *The Vancouver Sun*, *The Georgia Straight*, *The Capilano Review*, *The Martlet, filling station, Geist*, sub-TERRAIN, *Dig, broken pencil*, and all the other musicians, artists, writers and patrons who support the Lung by buying our books and attending our launches. All the best.